SABBATH

SABBATH

dan b. allender

Published in Nashville, Tennessee, by Thomas Nelson. Thomas Nelson is a registered trademark of Thomas Nelson, Inc.

Page Design by Casey Hooper.

Thomas Nelson, Inc., titles may be purchased in bulk for educational, business, fund-raising, or sales promotional use. For information, please e-mail SpecialMarkets@ThomasNelson.com.

Unless otherwise noted, Scripture quotations are taken from the *Holy Bible*, New Living Translation. © 1996. 2004. Used by permission of Tyndale House Publishers, Inc., Wheaton, Illinois 60189. All rights reserved.

Scripture quotations marked NIV are taken from HOLY BIBLE: NEW INTERNATIONAL VERSION®. © 1973, 1978, 1984 by International Bible Society. Used by permission of Zondervan Publishing House. All rights reserved.

Library of Congress Cataloging-in-Publication Data
Allender, Dan B.
  Sabbath / Dan Allender.
    p. cm.
  Includes bibliographical references.
  ISBN 978-0-8499-0107-2 (hardcover)
  1. Sunday. 2. Rest—Religious aspects—Christianity 3. Sabbath. I. Title.
  BV111.3.A44 2008
  263'.3—dc22
                          2008037265

Printed in the United States of America
09 10 11 12 QW 5 4 3 2 1

To my Naver River fishing friends—
Sabbath rhythms, tight lines.

Andrew Allender, Stan Bogden, Matthew Carucci,
Ron Carucci, Tracey Dean, Andy McCoy,
Matt McCoy, Mike McCoy, Stan Smartt

CONTENTS

CONTENTS

FOREWORD

THE ABRAHAMIC FAITHS OF JUDAISM, CHRISTIANITY, AND Islam share a common religious ancestry, not only in their claim to unbroken descent from the same patriarch but also in their adherence to a fixed set of seven religious concepts and practices, at least two of which were established before Abraham was even Abraham.

Each of the three communions has continued to retain those same seven over the centuries, even as each has spent centuries as well as enormous energy in enculturating them. The processes by which each faith group has adapted tithing, fasting, fixed-hour prayer, Sabbath observance, adherence to the liturgical year, sacred pilgrimage, and participation in the sacred meal to accommodate the ways of their own varying cultures makes for some intriguing moments in religious history; but none of the seven has enjoyed so rich or varied a genesis as has that of the Sabbath and its proper observance.

Interestingly enough, the discipline of keeping one day holy unto the Lord is the only one of the Abrahamic practices that is commanded as such. That is, of the seven, it is only Sabbath-keeping that was included at Sinai as a part of the decalogue or Torah. The question of just exactly what does and does not constitute proper Holy Day observance likewise has dominated religious conversation far more than has any concern with the other six practices. Sabbath, by whatever name and in whatever age, matters.

I think I did not really appreciate the depth of those circumstances—much less the implications of them—until I began to read the manuscript and permutations of manuscript that led to the book you now hold in finished form in your hands. Admittedly, the genius of this book lies in part in Dan Allender's obvious devotion to and belief in Sabbath keeping. Much of it undoubtedly lies also in the sheer breadth of his knowledge, as a professional theologian, about what he is talking about. But beyond those two things, informing as they obviously are, is Dan Allender's affection for something that he feels has shaped him and which he relays in these pages with a kind of intimacy that, at times, is almost poetry and is always affectionate.

I never thought of *shabbos* as a thing of delight before, never thought of it as a time for the soul to play and take its leisure, never before thought of it as a time of training for learning to walk again, as once we did, in familial communion with the Father. What has happened for me in working with this manuscript is a transposition of the Sabbath from rule and commanded observance to holy romp and secret playground where each visit only adds another level of delight.

Whether or not such a transposition will happen for all who read this book, I of course can not say. All I can say is that I am deeply grateful that it has happened for me, and I hope most earnestly it will be so for you as well.

Phyllis Tickle, General Editor

ACKNOWLEDGMENTS

I AM INDEBTED TO A HOST OF PEOPLE WHO BRING ME great joy:

First, to my publisher, Matt Baugher, who was once my agent—dear friend, bless you for thinking of me when this project became available. Your kind words have been a feast of delight. As well, to Sealy Yates—already your willingness to listen to my dreams is an immense gift.

To the Mars Hill Graduate School Sabbath class, including my glorious coteacher Rob Gillgrist—your hard questions, invaluable presentations, and joy in the Sabbath gave me courage and allowed me to test the content and tone of this material.

Thank you to Heather Abbott, Michael Audas, Erin Banasik, Justin Barrante, Tamara Bolding, Christy Broyles, Elise Cadwell, Carol Carson, Andrew Chamberlin, Rene Cline, M'Lyss Fruhling, Catherine Golden, Tracy Kouns, Lindsey Leitner, Patrick Love, Alison May, David Michalowski, Jessica Miller, Angela Kirby Nixon, Lisa Quinlan, Samuel Rainey, Joshua Reynolds, Christopher Roberts, Shannon Stauffer, Kathleen Stewardson, Carin Taylor, and Kelsie Thimsen.

To my dear friends, Pam Davis, Scotty Smith, and Elizabeth Turnage—thank you for your careful reflections, critique, and joy in offering your heart to me.

To Ron Carucci—your time helping me wrestle through

the unsettling questions that were the impetus to this book was invaluable, like all our labor.

To my young, gifted, and wise researchers, Phillip Nellis and Rachel Clinton—I cannot count the number of times I heard you make connections, ask questions, and offer thoughts that shaped this book. It was the rare experience with you: a delicious blend of academic, relational, pastoral, theological, and philosophical delight. Thank you, thank you. Your brilliant hearts and wise minds made this process a time of great play.

To my wife, Rebecca—it is odd, isn't it? Decades ago you invited me to receive the day, and I smiled and ignored you. How could you offer me such honor, delight, and courage after I let the gift reside on a shelf and missed your heart? I believe it is because you breathed Sabbath beauty and redemption until my exhaustion and emptiness necessitated change. I grieve it took so long; I celebrate that we have known a new kind of rest that I long to live until the eternal Sabbath breaks fully into this world. You, my love, are the delight of my days.

INTRODUCTION
Delight that Delivers Us to Joy

ONE NIGHT IN A REFUGEE CAMP IN THAILAND, A HALF-
mile from the Burma border, taught me what I most want to
say about the Sabbath. My wife and I were visiting the Mai
Sot camp, which houses fifty thousand refugees who fled from
the genocidal Myanmar government in order to study under
Dr. Simon, the president of a Bible college and seminary in
the camp. In the eighteen years he has been in exile from his
home in Burma, Dr. Simon has trained more than one thousand graduates from India, Burma, Thailand, Vietnam, Laos,
and Cambodia.

I spoke at a midweek church gathering of the Karen people
that lasted two hours with men, women, and children who sang
some of the most beautiful melodies I have ever heard.

After the service, we sat leisurely with Dr. Simon for three
hours. We ate simple, abundant, and delicious food and heard
the story of their glory and their suffering. During World War
II, the Karen people were selected by the British as royal sol-
diers and promised protection and honor for their service to the
crown. Instead, the British left Burma and refused to meddle in

the affairs of that decolonized nation. Soon thereafter, the ruling party began to steal their lands, violate the women, and kill their men. The devastating effort of the Myanmar government to wipe the Karen people off the earth—one of the least-publicized atrocities of the twentieth century—had begun.

Dr. Simon wove a story of profound horror, heartache, and hope that began with his father, a military officer, and his father-in-law, a general in the Burmese army. The night had long before turned ink black, except for the candles flickering on our table. The dance of light broke the darkness as the rhythm of his story progressed from personal past, to ancient tribal stories, to biblical themes, to current suffering and hope. There was nothing competing with the passage of the story— no e-mails to check, no cell phones to answer, and no tasks that demanded to be finished. In the background were the faint and staggeringly beautiful melodies of Christmas songs. The Karen people welcome the birth of Jesus by singing hymns and carols all night long, house to house, through their bamboo- and leaf-covered community.

There was the hush of the jungle, serenaded by crickets and frogs, and the breath of fresh air—cool, lush, and fragrant. Hours passed, but they seemed like only minutes. Dr. Simon said, "We will talk tomorrow if you'd like; I am ready for sleep." In an elegant and final transition, he blessed us and then went to bed.

My wife said it first: "We are in a holy place."

A HOLY DAY

Time, food, conversation, sorrow, hope, and companionship take on a rare, sweet, and compelling cast when one discovers holy time. "The earth is the LORD's" (Ps. 24:1), and all space is holy; yet not all space has been sanctified. But time—a single day, the Sabbath—is to be sanctified as holy.

The stories of God's presence that my wife and I heard in the refugee camp filled that domain with the marks of Christ's death, resurrection, and ascension. It was not merely a refugee camp, full of heartache and hatred, despair and hope; it was a place of breath and bone, blood and prayer. Seldom have I known space or time on this earth that was as holy as our time with Dr. Simon in that seminary.

Yet I am to know a time that is as holy and beautiful each and every week of my life. The holy is not located in one designated and agreed-upon space, such as a church, a monastery, or a stunning vista that captures a breathtaking view of a mountain range. The holy comes in a moment when we are captured by beauty, and a dance of delight swirls us beyond the moment to taste the expanse of eternity in, around, and before us.

The holy usually comes in unexpected, utterly surprising moments where the gift of goodness opens our heart to wonder and gratitude. It may come as we are traversing a familiar ski run and the play of light and shadow creates a stage of grandeur; or in awakening in your new home in Addis Ababa, Ethiopia, after six months of language study and realizing that for the first time you dreamed in the native language. These moments of delicious surprise are pregnant with delight.

The holy usually comes in unexpected, utterly surprising moments where the gift of goodness opens our heart to wonder and gratitude.

Delight doesn't require a journey thousands of miles away to taste the presence of God, but it does require a separation from the mundane, an intentional choice to enter joy and follow God as he celebrates the glory of his creation and his faithfulness to keep his covenant to redeem the captives.

What I learned from Dr. Simon is that Sabbath rest is entered when we refuse to be bound by complexity or drowned by despair. We enter delight only as we gaze equally and simultaneously at creation and redemption, in spite of the darkness that surrounds us and constantly clamors to be truer than God. How does Dr. Simon hold hope? I can't fathom how he remains steadfast after eighteen years in a refugee camp. His life exposes the counterfeit legions of ways we find solace and pleasure that we often think of as joy. His delight demands that I consider how little I know about delight.

The Sabbath is an invitation to enter delight. The Sabbath, when experienced as God intended, is the best day of our lives. Without question or thought, it is the best day of the week. It is the day we anticipate on Wednesday, Thursday, and Friday—and the day we remember on Sunday, Monday, and Tuesday. Sabbath is the holy time where we feast, play, dance, have sex, sing, pray, laugh, tell stories, read, paint, walk, and watch creation in its fullness. Few people are willing to enter the Sabbath and sanctify it, to make it holy, because a full day of delight and joy is more than most people can bear in a lifetime, let alone a week.

There are three core premises that will be engaged throughout this book. It will be immensely helpful for you to consider these assumptions as you enter the rest of this labor:

- The Sabbath is not merely a good idea; it is one of the Ten Commandments. Jesus did not abrogate, cancel, or annul the idea of the Sabbath. In the Ten Commandments, the fourth (Sabbath) is the bridge that takes us from the first three, which focus on God, to the final five, which concentrate on our relationships with others.
- The Sabbath is a day of delight for humankind, animals, and the earth; it is not merely a pious day and it is not fundamentally a break, a day off, or a twenty-four-hour vacation.
- The Sabbath is a feast day that remembers our leisure in Eden and anticipates our play in the new heavens and earth with family, friends, and strangers for the sake of the glory of God.

THE FOURTH COMMANDMENT

Few people begin the week boasting in how many lies they plan to tell in the next five days or end the week full of pride about how much loot they have stolen. We live in a dark day, but it is still rare for someone to publically tout his or her violation of the Ten Commandments, with one exception—our debasement with busyness. We love to tell others how much we work, how much we still have to get done, and how overwhelmed we are with the exhaustion of our labor. We admire busyness, speed, and productivity, yet we envy those whose leisure time is abundant. We are mad, crazy mad—and we know it. To write another book on the need for margins seems at best superfluous and, at worst, avoiding what most needs to be said: Sabbath rest is not an option; it is a commandment.

Sabbath rest is not an option; it is a commandment.

No one likes to be told what to do. In fact, I find it fascinating that, in my reading of many, many books and articles on the Sabbath, few begin with the fourth commandment as a premise. Instead, we are often told to practice the Sabbath because it is good for us. And it is. But first, ponder this thought: it is as wrong to violate the Sabbath as it is to steal, lie, and kill. Of course, there are varying consequences for violating any of the Ten Commandments. Having an affair may cost you your marriage, but it will in most cultures not cost you your life. Stealing a pencil from work doesn't bring the same consequence of jail time as stealing a car.

It is, nevertheless, wrong to violate the Sabbath. We are to sanctify the day and keep it holy. God commands us to obey him because he is our Creator, and he has authority to set the parameters of how we will live in his creation. If we violate his normative structure, there will be consequences that spiral through all dimensions of life.

If we could only see the ramifications of our rebellion, we would flee from our sin. But seldom is breaking God's law experienced as foul; it seems either necessary and/or beneficial. We seldom see sin, at first sight, as what it truly is—ill and deforming. Imagine if someone were to offer you the opportunity to take a deep breath of fresh Rocky Mountain air on a cool August morning or the choice to inhale a cloud of dark, oily diesel exhaust fumes. Every time we turn from God, we inhale the dark fumes of diesel fuel.

A commandment is often assumed merely to be a prohibition. Such thinking is idiocy. God's commandments prevent us from sucking diesel fumes in order to orient us to delicious, fresh air. Sabbath is the healthiest air for us to breathe, and it requires we obey God's command and turn from anything less desirous. And here is the rub.

Many who take the Sabbath seriously and intentionally ruin it with legislation and worrisome fences that protect the Sabbath but destroy its delight. For many Sabbath keepers, it is a day of duty, diligence, and spiritual focus that eschews play and pleasure for Bible reading, prayer, naps, and tedious religious services that seem designed to suck the air out of the soul. If that is keeping the Sabbath holy, then it is better to break it. The darker option is to ignore it, or perhaps even worse, to think one is keeping it simply by going to church. For many, the Sabbath has somehow morphed into Sunday, the day of the resurrection, and it is fulfilled by attending a religious event called Sunday morning church service. Once that is finished, the day is spent in routine yard maintenance, diversion, and preparation for the coming week. It cannot be shouted louder from the rooftops: This is not a Sabbath! This is Sabbath-breaking.

Many who take the Sabbath seriously and intentionally ruin it with legislation and worrisome fences that protect the Sabbath but destroy its delight.

Does the Sabbath have to be exactly twenty-four hours? Must it be celebrated on Sunday or on Saturday? Could it begin on Saturday a half hour before dusk and end Sunday at near the same time? These questions too often take us far from the true heart of what it means to celebrate the Sabbath. The Sabbath is simply not a day to "perform" religious activities and then to claim the rest of the day for thoughtless routine or mere entertainment or diversions.

It doesn't matter what day you enter the Sabbath. Many

who minister in our churches as pastors may celebrate the Sabbath on Monday or Friday; in fact, most who work in the church live in the endless cycle of religious tedium and chronic exhaustion. The issue is not when or how long, but if a day is at all chosen for delight.

Many who take the Sabbath seriously and intentionally ruin it with legislation and worrisome fences that protect the Sabbath but destroy its delight.

If we begin with the premise that the Sabbath is not merely a good idea or an option for how to spend one day a week, but that it is also God's holy commandment—then we can ask why we do not enter the day with intentionality and joy. What does it mean to sanctify the day as holy?

DAY OF DELIGHT

Imagine someone came to you and said, "Dream delight for yourself and your family and friends. Let yourself go with dreams as wild as you can imagine. Don't let money or physical limitations enter your thoughts. Dream as extravagantly as you know how to do, then pray that you might truly dream well. Where would your dreams take you? Where would you go, with whom, and what would you do?

Notice your reaction to the above invitation to dream about delight. Many students in my Sabbath class have said:

- "That is simply not realistic, and there is no point to make myself miserable by acknowledging what I want and can't have."
- "Don't you think the question says more about your social status and success than it does a biblical invitation?"
- "How do you dream delight when you are struggling with money and exhaustion?"
- "Delight is too subjective. What delights me may not be moral or the right thing to do on Sunday."
- "When I think of delight, I get sad and I want to eat more."

Like many of these students, the idea of dreaming delight for myself terrifies and, at times, irritates me. I like it when it happens, but I usually don't like dreaming and planning delight, unless it is for someone else.

Dream as extravagantly as you know how to do,
then pray that you might truly dream well.

For example, I planned my wife's fiftieth birthday party for more than two years. It involved a cast of old friends, a trip to Europe, a replaying of her postcollege sojourn with dear friends through countless world capitals when I wrote her daily and slowly won her heart to marry me. It was a surprise gift that became more expensive and complex as each person brought his or her creativity to the drama. By the time it actually happened, more than a hundred people knew of our plans and celebrated my wife's milestone. I still recall the intricate labor with joy. But all the effort was for her, and I love to bring delight to my wife.

You may differ, but I believe that, to some extent, we are all troubled by delight. We are not averse to pleasure escapes or vacations. To vacate is to empty—that is, to get rid of something. When we vacate or take a vacation, we are not merely taking time off from work; we are flushing away the cares of the world as we indulge in the diversions of our empty space. We lie on the beach and dab ourselves with sun lotion, put in our iPod earpieces, and read the latest best-selling adventure story. This is not a Sabbath; it is vacating our work in order to fill ourselves with passing pleasure.

Many modern-day "vacations" have the allure of cotton candy—a brightly colored candy puff on a paper stick that promises a feast of fullness and is nearly impossible to eat without sticky compromise. Once we tear into the sugary diversion, it disappears in a flash and offers no substance. It is not enough, and it doesn't satisfy, even for a minute. The end only increases the desire for more—it doesn't bring awe or gratitude. This is the energy of consumerism, the heartbeat of a self-serving capitalism. The powers and principalities of consumerism demand we taste diversionary breaks that intensify our hunger for more goods rather than a Sabbath rest that brings us a taste of genuine good.

Perhaps one of the most radical gifts we can bring the developing Third World and the decaying Western society is the

Sabbath. Not a day off, but a day of celebration and delight. The Sabbath is a day when the kingdom to come has come and is celebrated now rather than anticipated tomorrow. It is a fiction, a theater of a divine comedy that practices eternity as a present reality rather than a future state.

Sabbath is not about time off or a break in routine. It is not a minivacation to give us a respite so we are better prepared to go back to work. The Sabbath is far more than a diversion; it is meant to be an encounter with God's delight.

The Sabbath mimics God's response on the seventh day; certainly he was not tired from his busy creational enterprise.[1] If we need to get downtime or chill, then we should use another day and not the Sabbath. In fact, if we enter the Sabbath with joy, then it will spill its abundance into the other six days, thus keeping us from indulging in idolatrous overwork that leads to even more intense indulgence in riotous pleasure. The Sabbath is the kind of delight that leads to life.

FEASTING SABBATH

This introduction was written in an orphanage that has morphed into a conference grounds on the outskirts of Addis Ababa in Ethiopia. I was speaking at a conference with dear friends Jan Meyers, Ron Carucci, and my wife to Ethiopians who help prostitutes and trafficked girls and women. And I just found out for the second night in a row we are having what the cooks thought to be what Westerners would want to eat. Last night was spaghetti with meatballs, and tonight is hamburgers. The Ethiopians are ecstatic. The four Westerners are despondent.

The difficulty in most all conversations is culture. Our hosts asked the cooks to prepare food they assumed we'd prefer. The cooks are operating out of kindness and presumption. The presumption is that we prefer our Western food—even more, that we would not really want to eat their native food.

I approached our host, Wonde, who speaks flawless English, and explained that if hamburgers were the only option we would eat them with gratitude, but if there was any possibility of getting Ethiopian food, we would gladly pay out of our pocket double or triple what we were paying for the hamburgers.

I love Wonde. We have interacted on many matters over several years, and I trust him like a brother. He smiled his wise and winsome smile and said, "I will see what I can do."

He beckoned me over and, in front of the chief cook, told me, "Tell her what you want. She doesn't believe me." I looked at her and explained, "I don't want to be offensive, but if there is any way possible to eat Ethiopian food, especially *injera*, then we would be most honored." She smiled, somewhat disbelieving but obviously thrilled. She said in Amharic to Wonde, "They can eat what we fix for ourselves tonight. Is that acceptable?" He translated, and I said the only other word I know in Amharic— *qonjo*, which means both delicious and beautiful. We invited the cook to eat with us and shared a great preliminary feast in the mile-wide smiles on both our faces. No five-star fare is a feast if eaten alone or eaten in silence or banality with another. To be fully enjoyed, a meal must be eaten in communion with others, including the rich diversity of God's creation and redemption.

A feast is a rhythm of listening and learning together. A feast is a ritual or remembrance that involves food, music, dancing, and stories; we remember the time when we dined with God in the garden, and we anticipate the day when we will dine with God in the new heavens and earth.[2]

Sabbath is a feast of remembrance and anticipation wrapped into a twenty-four-hour period of time. During the Sabbath, we are invited by God to celebrate with him in the cool of the day. Sabbath is far more like hanging out with God in a French café drinking an espresso and talking about Simone de Beauvoir and listening to cool jazz. If that sounds like torture to you, then Sabbath is more like a country fair pig roast after the judging of the calf competition. The day is sticky warm, yet the first coolness of the night is pressing out the heat and it is time to sit back and compare notes about who got the blue ribbon this year. A fiddle begins its compelling tune. It is about good food, drink, music, conversation, and the remembrance of sitting with God in the garden.

Sabbath is our re-creating the garden and recreating in the new heavens and earth.

This book invites you to consider the Sabbath from its ancient roots to its current practice. We will reflect on a theology of time, play, feasting, and delight. It may be intriguing to you, but it will be worse than useless unless you choose to at least experiment with the Sabbath. To read a book on the Sabbath and not enter the holy day is somewhat like waiting for an exquisite five-star meal and then forgetting to eat when it arrives because you were too busy chatting away on your cell phone. The way to make use of this book from the beginning is to ask the simplest question: what would I do for a twenty-four-hour period of time if the only criteria was to pursue my deepest joy?

What would I do for a twenty-four-hour period of time if the only criteria was to pursue my deepest joy?

These chapters will invite you to consider the following questions:

- Where and when have we experienced delight?
- Why do we so often flee from delight and lose the taste for it?
- What counterfeits turn our senses from joy?
- How do we begin to taste and see the goodness of God?

May we celebrate!

1

SELDOM SABBATH

SABBATH AS A TASTE OF THE PLEASURE OF GOD BEGAN for me with a six-month sabbatical several years ago. A friend, who knew that at the time my weekly Sabbath practices were shoddy at best—in reality, like a garden gone to weed—told me, "Normally, God only allows you to take on the large after you have been found faithful with the small, but in your case, he has allowed you to do it backward."

It was an apt and prescient warning. If I didn't know how to practice Sabbath on a weekly basis, how would I make use of days upon days that stretched out for six months?

> *If I didn't know how to Sabbath on a weekly basis, how would I make use of days upon days that stretched out for six months?*

My wife and I left a week after our youngest son was delivered to college to go to New Zealand for three months. We bought (okay, I bought) a motorcycle and proceeded on a three-month binge of fly-fishing and motorcycling through one of the most beautiful countries in the world.

It rained every day but five. We faced tempestuous winds that blew us hither and yon, and after many harrowing adventures we (okay, my wife) chose to sell the bike and retool our last three months in another locale. We chose Prague and then returned to Seattle for Christmas to be with our children and to do our laundry before the second half of the sabbatical.

During that month, we discovered that our ancient and beloved dog, Maggie, had cancer. My wife was diagnosed with skin cancer on the first day of the New Year. And two weeks before we were to depart, her mother went into the hospital with congenital heart failure.

The second half of the sabbatical came to a skidding stop. The first half had been glorious fun, but it had not been restful or reflective. The second half was designed to read, pray, reflect, and do a few European side trips by rail. It would be cozy and slow. We had both anticipated the time with relish, and it now appeared to be over before it began.

We put Maggie down. Becky had surgery, and after a few days we flew to be with her mother. After a week with her, it was apparent to her family that we were helpful but not necessary for her care. The whole family urged us to proceed to Prague.

It was an agonizing decision, but we chose to go. We knew that at any moment, we might need to return. The choice to go—to Sabbath—in the face of uncertainty and struggle is the true war with Sabbath.

We often fail to create a day of delight because to do so compels us to stand against the division, destitution, and despair that often holds us captive the other six days of the week. If you read many of the other excellent books on Sabbath, a premise soon appears in the first chapter: We are driven, exhausted, and depleted. We were created for the refreshing and replenishing gift of the Sabbath. And we don't do so to our peril.

If we would only take a weekly Sabbath, our lives would be more balanced and buoyant. Some books go so far as to say the Sabbath is the way God intended for us to recharge our batteries so we can return to work with more vigor. But we are either addicted to the pace and the power of our frenzy, or we are ignorant of God's blessed call to rest. In either case, seldom do we hear or consider heeding the fourth commandment. And why do we choose to disobey one of God's Ten Commandments?

WHY DON'T WE OBSERVE THE SABBATH?

In preparation for this book and a class I teach at Mars Hill Graduate School, I asked students to answer a brief questionnaire about their Sabbath practices and convictions. What I found didn't surprise me; the results simply reflected other conversations I've had during the last year.

Only four out of thirty students say they practice Sabbath. Those four vary in their practices, but one day every week—usually Sunday, except for the two who work in a church—is set aside as an intentional Sabbath. Of the other fifty-six students, 90 percent view the concept of the Sabbath as simply another word for *church*. Seventy percent view the Sabbath as a day of rules and regulations that focus far more on what we aren't to do, while they believe the focus of what we are to do is to be spiritual, pious, and God-focused.

In response to the question, If you don't observe the Sabbath, what do you suppose has kept you from doing so?—the typical answer was, I'm too busy. It would infringe on my work, schoolwork, socializing, and free time. One person wrote, "I know I need to chill out and get a break, but something always comes up on Sunday and I tend to let the demands of what I've not finished last week pile up to get done that day." Sabbath, if it is considered at all, is a break, a down day to rest. And as much as we know we need rest, we also know that we need to tie up the last week and prepare the canvas for the week ahead.

As Americans, we tend to be proud, distracted, and afraid. And the greatest of these three is fear.

PRIDE

Not long ago, I was on a ferry between our home and Seattle and heard another man greet a friend. He said, "How are you, Bill?" His friend replied, "I'm so busy I won't be able to dig out of this morass for a month." His friend replied, "I know what you mean; I had over a hundred e-mails come in by ten o'clock this morning." Boasting about work is a national pastime. The one who works harder, against greater odds, and with fewer resources to gain the greatest ground wins. We are proud that we shoulder such immense responsibility and push our plow with the pride of aristocracy. Sabbath yanks us off our high horse, and for that reason alone few wish to dismount.

Pride metastasizes to the degree we prize power and presume that it is our possession to be used as we wish. The pride in never-ending work and in the power to shoulder Herculean demands has an even darker side. The proud, exhausted work addict believes he can cheat the fate of Sisyphus. In Greek mythology, Sisyphus was condemned to the endless cycle of drudgery and futility of pushing a boulder up a mountain, only to have it slip from his hands to tumble down the mountain— and then to begin the process again, for eternity.

The dark side of pride is that the work addict secretly believes he can outmaster the fates and find a way to achieve what others have failed to do. Somehow he will get his dream to remain on the top of the mountain and not slip from his grasp. Like any addiction, pride spins us deeper into the bondage of slavery, requiring other diversions to keep us from facing our plight.

DISTRACTIONS

We are also easily distracted. We are often like a child watching a circus—we are surrounded by too much drama. How do we choose what to focus on when the whole sea of activity begs to be taken in at once? If we choose to watch one clown, we may miss the activity in the other ring. Soon nothing is seen, because our senses close down when we attempt to take everything in.

When it comes to the Sabbath, the distractions often look something like this: Sunday afternoon, you receive a panicked call from a colleague whose portion of the report has to be done by Monday. He didn't realize he would need data until he began the report on Sunday morning. Can you help? It's work. But it's also friendship. And after all, it's just Sunday.

If it is not a colleague, then perhaps it will be your son or daughter who pleads to go to a neighbor's house after church or to a huge sale at a nearby store. Or the big game is on at 1:00 p.m., and you want to kick back and chill out for a few hours. What is so compelling about the Sabbath to miss a game, an opportunity to shop, to help a colleague, or drive your son or daughter to a friend's house? For most of us, nothing is compelling enough, unless we have bound ourselves to a set of legalistic rules about what we won't do on the Sabbath.

Often the defense against distractions is rigidity. We say that distractions are like Vanity Fair and can only be managed by a flintlike determination. We don't shop on the Sabbath—ever. We don't drive on the Sabbath—unless we are going to church. It is not okay to exchange money on the Sabbath, but polluting the earth with carbon-based fuels is just fine as long as the only driving is to church and back. We invent rules that seem orderly and sensible, if not righteous and moral, so that anyone who violates our code is somehow less than committed.

It is not hard to see why Sabbath has been consumed in Sunday church attendance. If we go to church, then we think we've fulfilled the fourth commandment. Once we leave Sunday worship, the day is ours, but it is best if there is some family time, downtime, spiritual time, and perhaps some leisure, or at worst, some work in the yard.

Is church attendance meant to be part of our Sabbath? It certainly depends on when you celebrate the day and when you attend church. Church service and Sabbath practice may be overlapped or distinct. Participation in a community of believers that regularly celebrates the table of the Lord, grows together in wisdom, and serves the poor of spirit and body is God's delight. But so is the practice of Sabbath. If one does enter the Sabbath over the same period as church participation, then it must be presumed that the church one attends brings immense pleasure and delight to the heart.

If the category of delight is used to assess our participation in church, I fear many would be compelled to acknowledge they "do their duty" and seldom enter the delight of God. There are countless factors for the onerous compulsion to attend church, just as there has always been an equal number of reasons not to attend; yet we are meant to know delight when we worship with others whom we know, care for, and delight in as we share together in the sacraments, Scripture, and suffering and joy.

I asked a friend, who would classify himself as someone who regularly attends church and confessess he desires to have Jesus at the center of his life, how he spent the Sabbath. He responded to me in an e-mail, tagging his day in bullet points:

- Good coffee, breakfast, e-mail, newspaper
- Sunday school, worship service, parking lot conversation
- Fast-food lunch, drop kids off at friends, shopping
- Football game, e-mail, two phone conversations with sound down
- Nap
- Walk with wife, talk to neighbors
- Read Henri Nouwen book
- Leftovers for dinner
- News and *60 Minutes*
- Work on Monday's schedule
- Early to bed

I asked him how he felt about the day, and he said it had been marvelous. He only wished he had had more time to pray and to talk with his kids, but he often feels that way and life is what it is.

The day my friend calls a Sabbath is merely a day (mostly) off from the mundane and pressured realities of work. It is not a bad day or a day ill used; it is merely pleasant. It is even possible that a glorious Sabbath might include each element of how he spent the day. But for my friend the day was just a break, not a Sabbath. What is the difference?

My friend's day was merely time off from work. Eugene Peterson calls this version of a Sabbath a "bastard Sabbath."[1] Weekends in America are, for many, a secular Sabbath that misses the glory of what God has called us to enjoy. Is it that we are too busy to enjoy the day? On the surface, that excuse is the most common I hear for not choosing to Sabbath. But I suspect there is something more than busyness that keeps us from the day.

FEAR

We are far more than distracted from our observance of the Sabbath; we are afraid. When asked, "What keeps you from observing the Sabbath?" two out of the sixty students I surveyed said, "I don't know what to do with a day that is meant to be full of delight." One person added, "Sabbath scares me because I am so much more comfortable with work, not play. I don't know what to do with joy." We are afraid of joy—and the Sabbath is welcoming God as our host who intends to bless us with delight on this day.

Many of us are afraid of delight. It seems to stand in such contrast to our harried multitasking. It is easier to drop exhausted before the television, laptop in hand, checking e-mails as we watch a pundit rattle on about the day's news, than to live in accord with a pace that is measured by delight.

Many of us are afraid of delight.

Are we doing what brings us delight, or are we merely doing what is expected if we are to keep our lives on the path we are on—the path that, honestly, we don't want? If asked at any one moment, "Are you experiencing joy?" most of us would be befuddled or irritated.

Delight stands counter to grief. There is so much uncertainty and loss in our lives, from the death of a parent to the rising cost of gasoline. To consider what delights us is to stand accused by the countless moments of onerous obligation and unfulfilled dreams. Instead, we would rather settle for distraction than open our hearts to what seems beyond our wildest dreams. We have learned to manage our disappointment with God, and we don't want our desire for delight to seduce us again.

Nothing is more desperately needed in our day than the Sabbath. It is not because we are driven, stressed, and exhausted. We are all those things. And if we practiced the ancient art of Sabbath, we would be incalculably less harried. However, our awareness of the need doesn't seem to be moving many, if any, to reconsider the Sabbath. As much as I concur with my Sabbath-writing colleagues who emphasize our need for rest, these writings fail to address what I believe to be the far more substantial issue.

We are driven because our work brings us power and pride that dulls our deeper desire for delight.

We are far more practiced and comfortable with work than play. We are far better at handling difficulties than joy. When faced with a problem, we can jump into it or avoid it; we can use our skills or resources to manage it. But what do we do with joy? We can only receive it and allow it to shimmer, settle, and then in due season, depart; leaving us alive and happy but desiring to hold on to what can't be grasped or controlled.

Joy is lighter than sorrow and escapes our grasp with a fairylike, ephemeral adieu.[2] Sorrow settles in like a 280-pound boar that has no intention of ever departing. One calls us to action and the other to grace. Which is easier: to work for your salvation with the self-earned power of self-righteousness or to receive what is not deserved or owed, but freely given and fully humbling?

Humanity is not made for Sabbath; Sabbath was made for all God's creation: male, female; slave, free; Jew, Gentile; believer, unbeliever; beast of burden, and the ground itself.[3] And Sabbath is not merely the cessation of work; it is turning from work to something utterly different from what we normally call rest.

SABBATH REST

In many ways, the problem with Sabbath is our understanding of the word *rest*. On the seventh day, God rested; and on the same basis as God, we are to rest. The Bible says, "So the creation of the heavens and the earth and everything in them was completed. On the seventh day God had finished his work of creation, so he rested from all his work. And God blessed the seventh day and declared it holy, because it was the day when he rested from all his work of creation" (Gen. 2:1–3).

The word "rested" is, without question, prominent in this passage. God rested on the seventh day of creation, yet it should be obvious that God rests not because he was weary from his labor. In this sense, *rest* must have a meaning other than taking a well-deserved break to stoke the fires for the next creative output.

Further, rest doesn't necessarily imply a cessation of activity. The passage says God completed his work in heaven and earth at the end of the sixth day. But then a fascinating phrase appears in the next verse. It says, "On the seventh day God had finished his work of creation, so he rested . . ." When did he complete, or finish his work—the sixth day or the seventh? And if the seventh day, what did he create that was not part of the heavens and the earth, but wrapped the bow around it so the package was finished?

It is suggested by many Jewish commentators that God created *menuha* on the seventh day. *Menuha* is the Hebrew word for rest, but it is better translated as joyous repose, tranquility, or delight. "To the biblical mind *Menuha* is the same as happiness and stillness, as peace and harmony. . . . It is the state in which there is no strife and no fighting, no fear and no distrust."[4]

God didn't rest in the sense of taking a nap or chilling out; instead, God celebrated and delighted in his creation. God entered the joy of his creation and set it free to be connected but separate from the artist.

> *God entered the joy of his creation and set it free*
> *to be connected but separate from the artist.*

In many ways, God's rest on the seventh day of creation is paralleled by the birthing process and the period after birth, when the labor is finished yet the bonding begins. The mother and father gaze endlessly at their child, who is distinct from the parents because she is no longer merely in the mind and the womb of the mother, but external and separate. She is no longer solely in the imagination or deep in the womb; she is finally released to be held in the arms of the parent. This attachment brings mother and child into a bond that, if secure, will last through thick and thin, heartache and loss, and provide the child with an assurance that all will be well.[5]

Similarly, God gazes in rapture at his creation and says, "She is so beautiful." We do not know what else God did or didn't do on the seventh day, but we can assume that his gaze did not vary or his delight wane as the day progressed. Instead, his infinite delight grew in wonder and joy as he surveyed all he created and declared that it was good.

No wonder we are so afraid of the Sabbath. It is nearly impossible to believe that God wants us to have a day of wonder, delight, and joy. It is more than unbelievable; it is often a burden to consider the Sabbath as a play day with God and others. As much as we may clamor for joy and freedom, when offered, it is often too painful to receive and to celebrate. In part, the pain is because we know our momentary dance will not last. It is easier to hold on to sorrow than to let go of joy.

If that is not hard enough, I must enter and then let go of joy before the face of the other six days. For six days, I wrestle with a world under the toil of the curse, soiled by the oil of humanity's commerce, deeply longing for the bright wings of the coming dawn. And each day, at best, is a repetition of the day before, unless the next day is the Sabbath. It is the queen of all days, the day in which division, destitution, and death are put aside to celebrate our union with God, the abundance of his love, and the wild hope of the coming kingdom. It is a day of holy fiction, a day when the promise of God is fulfilled on a stage where we write the script and take the roles we most want to act for his glory.

I offered this vision of the Sabbath to a small gathering of students, and the response was intrigue and irritation. One student bluntly said, "This messes with every notion I have ever had about the Sabbath. If it is true, then why wouldn't we live with greater anticipation?" Another added quickly, "It freaks me out. If I'm supposed to know what will bring me and others that kind of joy, then I wouldn't know how to fill one day, let alone fifty in a year, and then do so year after year. It is too much." The class came to a hush when someone else said, "I can't imagine that God would want such goodness for me. I know that is called grace, but I never thought it was supposed to be part of my week as a regular experience." We seldom think of Sabbath as a structure that mediates grace throughout creation.

SEEING GOD'S PLAN WITH NEW EYES

On the second half of our six-month sabbatical, my wife and I were in the quandary of not yet considering the Sabbath, or a sabbatical, as a gift of delight. To go to Prague meant leaving her ailing mother in the care of her siblings and choosing to rest, read, reflect, and play. Both of us felt guilty. It would have been easier if her siblings had said, "Stay. We can't do this without you." To go meant to depart the six-day world for the seventh; and to enter the seventh with a sanctity that put boundaries between the last day of the week and the first workday of the next. It meant that we were privileged to play when others were working to enable us to do so. The Sabbath is routinely rejected because it is one of our most profound tastes of grace.[6]

How does one celebrate joy when it is so dangerous? How does one do so when it is so foreign and demanding? And how does one celebrate the Sabbath when the sorrow and toil of the work week past and the coming week is standing on the boundary of the Sabbath and calling out for our undivided attention?

Our war is not with exhaustion and our driven obeisance to work—those battles are related but mere consequences of the deeper war. Our war is against the possibility that God truly desires for us the kind of delight and joy that would make our silly obsession with work look like futzing over an airline bag of peanuts when outside our window is Mount Rainier, in all her winter glory, waiting for the passenger to look and gasp in amazement.

The only way we can make use of the Sabbath with new delight is to see God's plan for the day with new eyes. In this book, we will build a case for delight by looking at the Sabbath as a festival that celebrates God's re-creative, redemptive love. The festival involves four key components:

- sensual glory
- rhythmic repetition
- communal feasting
- just playfulness

Our task is to set the stage with the best content and story to enable you to write the characters and develop the plot to make the Sabbath a day of delight for you, your family, and community.

PART 1

SABBATH PILLARS

2

SENSUAL GLORY

WHEN YOU OPEN OUR FRONT DOOR AND COME INTO OUR house, you see an interior wall that has entryways on both sides and is open at the top. This is a gallery wall where my wife displays her reproduction cross-stitch samplers. In the front is an antique dry sink.

At the moment, this wall features pictures of our oldest daughter's wedding, a coffeepot, Coptic crosses, an icon from our recent trip to Ethiopia, candles, cloth, and a sprig of evergreen from a blown-down limb. It is a menagerie of objects, arranged with care, that tells multiple stories. It is installation art that most guests pass by without a notice, but it arrests my attention because I know the beauty of each object and the interplay of the stories.

It dazzles me. Each object, whether a picture or an Ethiopian coffeepot, takes me to the faces related to the pieces, and if I allow myself I could linger before the wall and worship.

The core of delight is our capacity to worship, to create and enter beauty as a reminder and anticipation of God's goodness.

The core of delight is our capacity to worship.

I can smell the coffee brewing in the pot that Tsirit, Wonde's wife, used in the coffee ceremony in Addis Ababa. I can see my wife sitting in a broken-down chair in our tiny living space at Michigan State, patiently moving the needle in and out of the cloth ten thousand times before the sampler was finished. Likely not one of our prized objects is worth more than a few dollars to anyone bidding on our scraps after we are off this earth, but to us it is a holy wall.

Whenever I enter another person's space, I search for beauty. I have been in single-wide trailers that felt like I walked into a Van Gogh painting. I have been in multimillion-dollar homes that felt plastic and hollow. Beauty cannot be purchased from a catalog or selected by the most sophisticated designers; holy beauty must be crafted from material that is loved.

The Sabbath is a day in which we enter time and call it holy. We are far more apt to speak about space as holy. The wall I referred to is special, yet the beauty of the space is not fundamentally in its physical properties but in its capacity to translate me to the time and faces related to each object. It is, even more, the linkage between times as distant as a cross-stitch done thirty years ago while we were in seminary and a cross

from a recent trip. The wall talks to me of wonder, mystery, an
glory.

Holy simply means set aside, not lost in the sea of every
thing else. The holy is distinct in that it stands out and shim
mers with the presence of something far more than itself. The
holy translates itself into something else while still remaining
what it is. The Sabbath is only a day, yet it is the gateway to
another eon that cannot be entered by any other door.[1]

We are to sanctify the Sabbath and make it holy. The fourth
commandment, the longest and most expansive of all ten,
says:

> Remember to observe the Sabbath day by keeping it holy.
> You have six days each week for your ordinary work, but the
> seventh day is a Sabbath day of rest dedicated to the LORD
> your God. On that day no one in your household may do
> any work. This includes you, your sons and daughters, your
> male and female servants, your livestock, and any foreigners
> living among you. For in six days the LORD made the heav-
> ens, the earth, the sea, and everything in them; but on the
> seventh day he rested. That is why the LORD blessed the
> Sabbath day and set it apart as holy. (Ex. 20:8–11)

This passage addresses two unquestionable, indisputable
issues related to the Sabbath: inclusivity and cessation. We will
address the issues of inclusivity elsewhere, but it needs to be stated

here: Sabbath is not only for the elite, the spiritual, or the wealthy; it is for all equally, including one's beasts of burden. The second issue in the command also demands our attention: labor ceases.

Holiness requires separation, a standing apart from all else. The Sabbath is marked by some moment in time when the clutter and congestion of sameness is released. It is like loosening the line between a sailboat and the dock. The boat has been packed, all the provisions are onboard, and everyone is ready for the moment of send-off. When the line that tethers you to the land has been loosened and thrown aboard, the bow pushed away from the dock, and the engines put in forward—the Sabbath has begun. You are in another realm.

The mandate to rest from our work during the Sabbath is so slight and innocuous that it is boggling to the mind to consider how quickly questions come about how to "do it right." Should the Sabbath begin on Friday at dusk, Saturday, or Sunday at sunrise? Does it need to be twenty-four hours, or could it be morning and a part of the afternoon? Can one drive a car? Get gasoline? Stop for takeout food? Deliver food to a sick friend? Shop online if no one is working? Answer a phone?

The war against delight rages the moment one puts the boundary between the Sabbath and all other time. The war involves guilt and shame-based demands that we "do it right" so no one can accuse our motives or deeds, including God. We think, *If I obey the rules, then not only can I not be accused, but I win the self-righteous "reward" of boasting in my rightness.* We may not

exercise that right, but in our perspective, we can at least store up our self-righteousness in an account to be withdrawn to pay the daily incurring debts of failure. We hate the demand of rules; we refuse the freedom of parameters that allow us nearly infinite room to play.

The Sabbath prohibition invites us to turn from the mundane, the daily grind, to a new world and day for entering goodness. What is to mark the day? The first element we will consider is sensuality.

SENSUAL HOLINESS

Somewhere along the way, there has been a tragic division between holiness and sensuality. It is the work of evil to divide, and it must be fought directly and sensually. God stood back from each day of creation and declared that it was good. God called what he saw beautiful in that everything he created revealed something different about his glory.

Creation is not God, nor is it merely an extension of the God presence; it is distinct and other. Yet in the diversity, complexity, depth, and mystery of creation, there is a gift of love that is tangible and sensual. David Bentley Hart writes,

Creation's being is God's pleasure, creation's beauty God's glory; beauty reveals the shining of an uncreated light. . . .

Creation is only a splendor that hangs upon that life of love and knowledge, and only by grace; it is first and foremost a surface, a shining fabric of glory, whose inmost truth is its aesthetic correspondence to the beauty of the divine love. . . . It is delight that constitutes creation, and so only delight can comprehend it, see it aright, understand its grammar. Only in loving creation's beauty—only in seeing that creation truly is beauty—does one comprehend what creation is.[2]

Hart draws a number of key concepts together. Creation reflects God's glory, which is before us like a surface fabric whose deepest weave is a gift of God's love. And the only way to take it in, even to a degree, is through a hermeneutic of delight. One must stand before creation in awe and with gratitude if one is to see, taste, smell, hear, and touch God.

Creation is not a concept; it is a work of art—like a fragrant and tasty stew, a roiling and radiant van Gogh, or a soft and tender touch of a mother—and it can't be known without sensual wonder.

Creation is like a complex and compelling tapestry that is woven with delicate, bold artistry. The more you stand before it, the more you see the craft and care; yet the whole is more than one can take in without becoming dizzy and disoriented. Instead, we focus on a flower pattern, and the colors and texture soothe and excite us. We can't help but take in more than the bud, so our gaze shifts to the whole bloom. Already, we know our grasp of the whole is overwhelming, and we persist. But such intensity requires we turn away, at least for a moment. Beauty is both what we crave and more than we can bear.

Beauty is both what we crave and more than we can bear.

We must have the courage to enter our deepest craving and to know that we can't bear such glory for long. And when we turn from the beauty that so intensely shines before us, we must turn away—to a lesser beauty, but to beauty rather than to unholy.[3]

As I mentioned in the introduction, my wife and I were among those invited to speak at a conference in Ethiopia to teach men and women who work with prostitutes and trafficked girls and women. It was one of the sweetest privileges I have known to teach men and women who risk their lives daily offering grace and care to people who are often viewed as the vilest dregs of society.

We wondered how we would end such a beautiful time with these wise, bold, and beautiful people. Jan Meyers suggested we do foot washing and end with communion. I have seldom washed someone's feet or had my feet washed. But the idea struck me with such force that it seemed like the only possible way to end our time together.

The dilemma with writing about this experience is that the time was so holy, intimate, and life giving that I find it hard to describe it without weeping. It may, at first seem immensely humble to wash someone's feet, but we chose to do so, in large measure, because we knew it was truly asking for the greatest blessing. We asked our brothers and sisters in Christ if they would permit us this honor, and they consented.

Becky and Jan and I knelt before three large basins. One by one, the women came to Jan and Becky, and I washed the feet of the men. One man in particular, Jacob, came with reluctance. When I took off his shoes and spoke to him about his life, courage, and love, he could not look me in the eye. Jacob had worked for the president of his country when he was called of God to leave his prestigious job and to work in this ministry to prostitutes.

One year prior, he had been heartbroken by a missions organization that would no longer support him because he didn't have a Western presence to supervise his work. The missions group was concerned that Jacob might not use the funds with wisdom, given his propensity to give the money away rather than using it for his own benefit.

His heartache was not with the mission or their decision. His heartache was that he could no longer provide as much for the sixteen prostitutes who live in his home along with his wife and two children. He had come to question the possibility of trusting white Western men.

I washed Jacob's feet tenderly and long. The longer I swirled the water over his calloused, aging feet, the more I wept. He also began to weep. After I finished, I stood to hug him, and he began to sob in my arms. I have no idea how long we stood; I only know that something was freeing in both of us through our tears.

The Bible tells us, "How beautiful . . . are the feet of the messenger who brings good news" (Is. 52:7). Maybe you like feet, but I found them one of the least attractive parts of the body—until that night. Feet that bring the gospel are fleet and elegant. The paradox, I believe, is quite intentional. The Bible takes what is the least attractive and turns it into the height of beauty. It is simply a wonder. Will I ever know a more beautiful moment on this earth? Will I ever know honor and celebration as rich as I experienced that night?

I can hold the memory of that beauty in my mind only for so long, and then I must turn away. It is too bright, too full of everything that my life longs for and yet so seldom knows. It was beauty at its zenith, a taste of the delight of the Sabbath.

The height of our greatest moment of glory is but the doorway into the privilege of the holy tabernacle of time. My moments with Jacob were the doorway into my current delight in writing. I lit a candle. I knelt before I wrote and prayed along with the sonorous artistry of Yo-Yo Ma, who offered as part of my prayer Bach's Cello Suite no. 1 in G. I rose and stared out the window at the feast of gray colors surrounding my Seattle view. I lit a pipe with dark Scottish tobacco and settled to reread a portion of Ruth Haley Barton's *Sacred Rhythms*.[4] My heart is full, and Sabbath is only four hours away.

We are to bask in beauty, to surround our senses with color, texture, taste, fragrance, fire, sound, sweetness, and delight. And if we are to do so, each and every day, with joy, then how much more are we to do so on the Sabbath, when God stood back and marveled at his own creation?

Creation is good, and it yearns, cries out, and waits for its full glory to return. We are told by the apostle Paul that creation eagerly awaits its glorious day of freedom from death and decay (Rom. 8:21).

Creation is good, yet it groans. It needs a Sabbath as surely as you and I do. The Sabbath needs to be entered with tenderness and care to be encountered with the delight of love. What part of creation will you love this Sabbath? What portion of reality will you enter with senses aroused, ready, and desiring a taste of goodness? What beauty will you receive and then give back as the praise and honor that is deserved?

What part of creation will you love this Sabbath?

SABBATH WORSHIP

Worship is our response to beauty as we offer awe and gratitude for the gift of goodness. I once stood in a ravine a few miles from the base of Mount Cook on the South Island of New Zealand. The wind was ripping at 40 miles per hour, and the suspension

SENSUAL GLORY

bridge I had just walked over was swinging wildly enough that it seemed too treacherous to cross.

The clouds covered the peak of Mount Cook, but its sheer beauty commanded stillness. I stood at attention only broken a few minutes later by a voice of a stranger. A man standing next to me said, "Isn't she incredible?" His presence irritated me, and I was about to grunt, "No kidding." Instead, I turned to look at him in the eye, and the words came out of my mouth before I could stop: "Are you asking me to confess?"

He looked perplexed. "What did you say?" I repeated my phrase, and he stammered, "No, I was just saying that this view of Cook is magnificent." My face softened and I asked him, "Were you not asking me to confess with you that we are standing before something utterly awesome and breathtaking?" I doubt he wanted to engage the madman he had encountered, so he simply said, "Yeah, I guess so." I asked him, "Whom do you thank for all this glory?" He looked even more perplexed.

It is never enough to encounter awe alone or with others. Awe takes our breath away, and a moment of wonder returns us to the childlike sensation of being small in the face of something—Someone—bigger. Awe is humbling. The absence of humility is a mark of decadence and narcissism. Yet to feel awe while alone, whether it is experiencing the rush that comes as we plunge down the face of a roller coaster, or seeing one of the great wonders of the earth, leads to pride.

Awe must propel us to gratitude. To whom will we give

45

thanks for the breathtaking beauty of Mount Cook, for the ingenuity to create the world's tallest roller coaster, for the fragrant wine we savor before we make love? It feels right, but insufficient to thank the big bang theory, a group of engineers, or even a vineyard and my wife. I was made for more. I was made to sing to the heavens the glory of God.

God asks Job, "'Where were you when I laid the foundations of the earth? . . . as the morning stars sang together and all the angels shouted for joy?'" (Job 38:4, 7). This is a disconcerting question. I don't know where I was. I didn't exist at the time of creation; of that I am aware. But to engage the Creator, I must be willing to be questioned and to enter a dialogue of wonder.

Worship as awe and gratitude is the stance of a childlike learner who with curiosity opens her heart to more and more desire to know. Not a knowledge that dissects and controls, but a holy knowing that is a union of sensual desire and satisfaction beyond our wildest dreams. Worship is a knowing that transforms us because we can barely take in the beauty, let alone speak to the Creator and hope to be heard. To say, "Thank you, thank you for including me in this moment," and then to hear the Creator say in return, "No, thank you for joining me in this glory, for celebrating with me my glory" is the truest essence of Sabbath.

Therefore, it is not enough to ask, what beauty will you enter this day of Sabbath delight? Instead, we must ask, what beauty will you explore and get lost in during this day of celebration? What beauty will open your eyes to the questions God wants you to ponder in order to increase your awe and gratitude?

The Sabbath is the day to experiment with beauty that teases your hunger to know more glory. It is a day of study and silence on one Sabbath, a cutting out of a new kite pattern to fly on a wild breezy Sabbath another. It is crawling through wetlands below your home like hunters stalking big game in Patagonia or an exploration of string theory and Heisenberg's uncertainty principle as it relates to quantum physics on the next. What intrigues, amazes, tickles your fancy, delights your senses, and casts you into an entirely new and unlimited world is the raw material of Sabbath.

The Sabbath is the day to experiment with beauty that teases your hunger to know more glory.

The only parameter that is to guide our Sabbath is delight. Will this be merely a break or a joy? Will this lead my heart to wonder or routine? Will I be more grateful or just happy that I got something done?

Delight requires the courage to be attentive, intentional, and diligent. It will not happen without planning and preparation. It requires I ask myself, and my spouse, and my children, and my friends, and others: What will bring us joy? We must be guided by creation to engage creation. Listen to the psalm:

Let the heavens be glad, and the earth rejoice!

Let the sea and everything in it shout his praise!

Let the fields and their crops burst out with joy!

Let the trees of the forest rustle with praise

before the LORD . . . (Ps. 96:11–13)

To listen and let the heavens and earth be glad, to hear the pounding of the sea and the crops burst out with joy and the trees rustle with praise requires, at the least, quiet. We must put ourselves before creation and listen. Open your senses and take in all that is moving before you. Quiet the questions as to why or even how. Silence the accusations or doubt. It will not serve us well if the Sabbath is entered, or even planned, in busyness.

All that is required is to know that God dances in his creation. Tune your senses to the play of God, and when you are ready, join in the Sabbath dance.

3

HOLY TIME

THE SABBATH HAS BEEN CALLED A "SANCTUARY IN time."[1] It comes at a distinct time and then departs. It has followed that rhythm every week from the first Sabbath to now, and it will continue to follow that rhythm until the moment when time will find its fulfillment in an endless Sabbath. The Sabbath is not merely an event that happens in time; it redefines the nature of time and how we are to live it.

> *The Sabbath is not merely an event that happens in time;*
> *it redefines the nature of time and how we are to live it.*

We will not be able to imagine how we are to live in time differently until we stand back and discover how we currently live in it. The Sabbath is the day that holds together the beginning of time and the end; it is the intersection of the past and future that opens a window into eternity each week.

How did we get to be so far from this way of seeing and celebrating the Sabbath?

TIME IS FLEETING

We live in a time-troubled era. We often indulge in overwork and end up overwhelmed and exhausted. More than half of those polled said being overwhelmed by the amount of work to be done in the previous month. One out of three reports they are chronically overworked.[2] As a result, more than half of white-collar workers log more than forty hours a week, and 75 percent of those who work more than forty hours do work on the weekend.[3]

Studies tell us that 37 percent of Americans take fewer than seven days off per year. Only 14 percent take vacations of two weeks or longer.[4] Americans take the shortest paid vacations in the world, and 20 percent of those who do take vacation days stay in touch with the office.[5] One study indicates, "Time has become a precious commodity and the ultimate scarcity for millions of Americans. A 1996 *Wall Street Journal* survey found 40% of Americans saying that lack of time was a bigger problem for them than lack of money."[6]

Many people experience time as an unruly mess that is often out of control. We *need* time, as if God has not allotted to us all that we are meant to have. We *make* time, as if we had the power to create it. We *steal* time, as if we could add more to our lives. We *spend and use* time, as if it really were a commodity.

Abraham Heschel writes, "Space is exposed to our will; we may shape and change the things in space as we please. Time, however, is beyond our reach, beyond our power."[7] We chafe at the thought that time is not under our control.

The assumption is that time is fleeting and we have to take hold of it; space—that is, the material world around us—is what seems permanent and real. Our perspective is upside down. Time is sure and solid, and we have no control over it. Heschel offers this befuddling language to put us right side up. He writes,

> Time, that which is beyond and independent of space, is everlasting; it is the world of space which is perishing. Things perish within time; time itself does not change. We should not speak of the flow or passage of time but of the flow or passage of space through time. It is not time that dies; it is the human body which dies in time. Temporality is an attribute of the world of space, of things of space. Time which is beyond space is beyond the division in past, present, and future.[8]

If Heschel is correct, time doesn't have to be redeemed or used or stolen or made or spent; instead, we are called to submit to time as the medium in which we live.[9] Time is simply to be breathed like air.

Time doesn't have to be redeemed or used or stolen or made or spent; instead, we are called to submit to time as the medium in which we live.

TIME IS A MACHINE

Early in the Industrial Revolution, the clock became the most transformative tool to turn humanity from an agrarian view of the rhythm of seasons and calendar to the power of precise, managed, and controlled time. "The clock, not the steam-engine, is the key machine of the modern industrial age."[10] Juliet Schor wrote,

> The first "capitalist" enclaves appeared in fourteenth century Europe where the textile industry responded to economic crisis by decreasing wages and extending working hours that were regulated by manually rung bells (early clocks). *Werkglocken* "signaled to workers when they should arrive at work, the timing of meals, and the close of the day. The idea was that the clock would replace the sun as the regulator of working hours. But unlike the sun, the clocks would be under the control of the employer."[11]

This transition has been so effective that we are unable to think of time as a created presence that is not a mechanism merely to be divided, sequenced, measured, and therefore ruled.[12] We seldom honor the reality that we own time; we are far more inclined to use time to gain advantage and control.

The oddity is that the more we treat time like an extension of a machine, called a clock, the more we are bound to time as if it is the boss and we are the slave. The proof of that is most people feel rushed and hurried along by time. Projects are crammed into brief windows of time. We move hurriedly from one task to another, decreasing margins and doing more. We reason that if we can *gain* time, then we can also *lose* time.

I was finishing another writing project as I worked on this book. I took several days while I was overseas to write. I wrote for four hours every day and was near completion, when on the way back I was interrupted by a meal service and the tray was put on my table before I could close my computer. I held my laptop above the tray and saved the document, and then closed the computer down. Apparently, I did something wrong. When I opened it after lunch, my entire document was gone. I did everything I knew to do to retrieve it, and there was nothing but a blank page. Irrespective of the cause, my first thought was, *I've lost all that time; when will I get the time to do it over? I have wasted precious time, and it is gone.*

Several deep presumptions exist in those sentences. *I own time; and it owns me. It is mine to use; and when I waste it, as if I could, it is my fault.* There was no thought that in rewriting the work, it may improve far more than a mere editing of the first document. Time is not lost or gained, spent or used—one can only do that with space: time can only be honored as a gift. When we see time as a machine, then when it appears to break, we can do little but vent our frustration and wait for the expert to help us, rather than to submit and honor the One who has created time for our delight.

TIME IS MONEY

If time is money, as Benjamin Franklin advised us, then it is just another commodity that can be consumed. And much of our struggle with time is the burden we bear as consumers. Alexander Schmemann exposes the darkness of our frenzied labor: "The joyless rush is interrupted by relaxation, but such is the horror of the strange vacuum covered by this truly demonic word, 'relaxation,' that men must take pills to endure it."[13]

We rush at great speed; and the faster we move, the less human we become. We become as much a commodity because all we have to sell to gain more resources, to have more leisure, is time. As Madeline Bunting writes, "The harder you work, the longer and the more intense your hours, the more pressure you experience, the more intense is the drive to repair, console, restore, and find periodic escape through consumerism."[14]

We ride this bullet at increasingly intense speeds. Speed becomes a drug that helps us escape seeing our empty, dull, time-addicted lives. David Whyte wrote,

Speed is the ultimate defense, the antidote to stopping and really looking. If we really saw what we were doing and who we had become, we feel we might not survive the stopping and the accompanying self-appraisal. So we don't stop, and the faster we go, the harder it becomes to stop. We keep moving on whenever any form of true commitment seems to surface. Speed is also warning, a throbbing, insistent indicator that some cliff edge or other is very near, a sure diagnostic sign that we are living someone else's life and doing someone else's work. But speed saves us the pain of all that stopping; speed can be such a balm, a saving grace, a way to tell ourselves, in an unconscious ways, that we are not really participating.[15]

It is a vicious cycle of disappointed desire or dissatisfaction, increasing the need to work more, to use and misuse time, to squander it as if it were a commodity to be spent. Time is to be submitted to, honored, and enjoyed. And all views of time that fail to do so are doomed to never receiving the Sabbath.

SABBATH RHYTHM

The Sabbath is weekly. It is to be anticipated and remembered, and while present, to be enjoyed and engaged. Sabbath provides a weekly marker for the contours of life. It is the moment to receive all time and to allow the past and future to congeal, to thicken into ripe, holy fermentation.

Sabbath provides a weekly marker for the contours of life.

To use another analogy, the Sabbath stands at the end of the week and at the beginning of the next as the bridge between past and future. Far more, it is the day that bridges two great events in time: creation by God and the re-creation of the new heavens and earth by God.

Sabbath was given to humanity before the fall of humanity into sin (Gen. 1) and as a commandment (Ex. 20, Deut. 5) that preceded the entry into the Promised Land, a sign of the new heavens and earth. Sabbath remembers creation and anticipates re-creation. It is an eschatological event that prefigures a sin-free, glory bound world. As we remember Eden in the Sabbath celebration, we also imagine and anticipate the renewed and redeemed garden that is to come.

Sabbath demands that we look at time from a different perspective than a linear, sequential, progressive process. The most commonly held view of time in the Western world was developed by Augustine. In his highly subjective view of time, the present doesn't exist—there is only the past and the future. The past is entered by memory and is spent, gone, and mostly regretted. The future cannot be known or remembered; therefore, its uncertainty causes us worry.[16] Time, for Augustine, is not a matter of joy; it is wearisome and hard.

There are many other views of time that compete with the Western perspective. For example, many African tribes see time as episodic rather than chronologically linear.[17] Consequently, keeping time is not the goal as much as being in the rhythm or the flow of time. In contrast, our Western view of time is static and geometrical. There are other people groups that see time as swirling and moving—the future being revealed in the past, and the past illuminating the future. In their noncontinuous view of time, the present is not cut off from the past and future; rather, it is a synthetic whole that spills over in all directions like an undulating wave.[18]

I suspect that most everyone knows the experience of being lost in time. Or perhaps better said, becoming so free in time (not from it) that the rhythm of our movement coincides with the heartbeat of time. It can be called a peak moment when we are utterly unselfconscious and merge with time, yet we become more ourselves in that moment than we could ever be as we check our watches.

Fly-fishing is a time dance for me. The rhythm of the rod and line, the sound of the passing water, the full-bodied concentration on eddies, slow water, rising fish, where my fly lands, and how it returns to me with or without drag takes me into a rhythm that allows time to pass with little awareness. I have been fly-fishing for six hours with no sense of time's passage, only an awareness of its goodness. Time has not so much progressed or stopped as it has allowed me to catch up and flow with it. The experience is exhilarating, and no matter how bone weary I am from the exertion, my soul feels young and carefree.

I can experience that as well in writing or reading. I have sat in libraries for ten hours reading Wittgenstein, understanding next to nothing, and yet aware I am walking at the same speed as time. Time and I are not at odds; we are not competitors, enemies, or even friends; we are lovers. I know those moments in sailing or in listening to friends talk about their passion, sorrow, and joy. We are meant to have many activities that allow us to walk with a fresh joy in pace with time; but we are only given one sanctified time, Sabbath, where the day is meant to be a unique entry into that rhythm.

The privilege to walk hand in hand with time doesn't come because you merely yearn for it or know it would be good for yourself and your family. It only comes to exist when time is sanctified and made holy. In the same way, fly-fishing was not a time dance for me at first; instead, it was like being whipped by my own rod and line, hung out to dry in trees and bushes, and falling headfirst into the water. I'm amazed to this day that given the agony of my first fly-fishing experience, I stuck with it. Learning to dance with the Sabbath is infinitely more important; therefore, it is far, far more difficult. It requires that we receive, intend, and protect the day.

RECEIVING THE DAY

The Jewish people refer to the Sabbath as the "queen." The word *sanctify* has the meaning of betrothal. We are betrothed to the "queen" of our hearts, and we are to prepare our homes for her arrival. We are to welcome her and to anticipate her arrival as the fulfillment of our deepest yearning. Heschel said, "To call it [Sabbath] bride is merely to allude to the fact that its spirit is a reality we meet rather than an empty span of time which we chose to set aside for comfort or recuperation."[19]

We can ruin the Sabbath by trying to make something of the day without opening our hearts to receive her coming. When we celebrate the Sabbath in a hospital with a dying friend, or after a night of nausea and flu, or on the road, the Sabbath is different than when we are well, happy, and at home. In all cases, we can celebrate the Sabbath, even in a fifteen-minute window, and receive the gift of the day.

All too often we approach the Sabbath like a forced conversation at a social gathering. People mill around on the deck, cup in one hand and snacks in the other; idle chitchat allows the time to pass. Seldom in a thousand gatherings have I had a meaningful or delicious conversation at a milling-about event. It is simply not the nature of the social beast. Chitchat is like junk food—it is quickly filling and often causes bloating. It is best handled in small doses.

When we approach the Sabbath as if it were a chitchat social gathering, we may have exquisite drinks and snacks, the deck spotless, and grill smoking with barbecue, but the experience will be little more than a nice gathering with warm greetings and spotless repartee, and not a feast where you hear "eternity utters a day."[20]

Receiving the Sabbath is like welcoming the day with the innocent and risk-taking heart of a child. Imagine what children feel on Christmas morning before they are set free to open their gifts. Their eyes beam. Their legs swing with abandon, and their bodies twitch with excitement. This is the day that "comes like a caress, wiping away fear, sorrow and somber memories."[21] How could we not be excited if we only allowed ourselves to suspend disbelief and enter the day as a delight?

INTENDING THE DAY

Welcoming a guest moves from the heart to the hands. We must polish the brass, wash the linens, and clean the floors before our houseguest arrives. How would you prepare your home if an honored guest was about to arrive? You would make all the necessary preparations with the joy of anticipation. No mundane activities would take your attention away from your guest's arrival.

We are not to work on the Sabbath because it takes us out of the play of joy. It is as bizarre as making love to your spouse, but getting out of bed during the process to cut your lawn or wash dishes. Such an offense would do far more than spoil the mood; it would be a direct assault on the integrity of joy, announcing that a mundane chore is more pleasurable than sexual joy with your spouse.

We are not to work on the Sabbath because it takes us out of the play of joy.

The things we do to prepare for the Sabbath may vary depending on favored rituals and plans unique to the day. But what it requires most of all is conversation with those who are part of your Sabbath. If you have invited friends to join you for part of the time, do they know that this is not a mere invitation to dinner but a joining of a Sabbath celebration? If a major trek in the mountains is in store, it will require that all the supplies are purchased and packed in the car before the Sabbath. If your family is going to play on the Sabbath by finger painting in the garage, then the garage needs to be cleaned and prepared before the play begins.

Preparation requires that we plan together, dividing tasks and joining together in making our homes a place of anticipation. For example, cooking a hearty and ample stew prior to the Sabbath can save the family from having to do any food preparation during the Sabbath. If part of your Sabbath celebration includes cooking a meal that involves the whole family, then someone has to purchase the ingredients before the day arrives.

The key word is *intentionality*. Joy doesn't just happen, nor is it served up on demand. Much as the notion that creativity is 10 percent inspiration and 90 percent perspiration, so Sabbath joy is part mysterious surprise preceded by much planning and preparation. The Sabbath calls us to receive and to create with God the delight he gives and invites us to orchestrate for his glory. It requires surrender and imagination.

Once the Sabbath ends, the next three days can be reflection, a remembering of the day, savoring what was sweet and reconsidering what might have made the day more glorious. There is righteous reflection that asks, how could the day have been better? This is not meant to be a laborious dissection but the pleasure of replanning the day, so as to better anticipate the Sabbaths ahead.

The three days before the next Sabbath can be the time when desires are discussed and a plan made. Obviously, plans can morph and change, yet the goal is not to create a straitjacket of demands and expectations but to prepare an unfettered path for one day.

PROTECTING THE DAY

Recently, I discovered I was prediabetic. My physician strongly encouraged me to lose weight to lower my fasting glucose number. I was afraid. I have friends who have suffered debilitating diabetes, and I was highly motivated to lose weight for the first time in my six decades on this earth.

I have tried to lose weight many times, but it was only fear that moved my heart to make radical changes. I gave up alcohol, sweets, and most painfully, all starch. I can still come unglued when I see a basket of bread in a restaurant. But I was motivated to make the requisite changes in my diet and lifestyle.

What I had not expected was how often friends and acquaintances (happily not my family) questioned if my total abstinence from alcohol, sweets, and starch was really necessary. Wouldn't moderation be a better course? Why couldn't I have one drink? "Just have a smidgen of this dessert. You'll love it," my well-intentioned friends would urge. I didn't take into account the level of resistance we face the moment we choose a course of action that bucks the trend of what others consider to be good, true, and lovely. Or better said, when we choose a course of action that exposes the lack of health in others, we can expect to be bombarded with temptation and, at times, contempt that questions our motives and sanity.

The same is true with regard to the Sabbath. The questions and, at times, contempt regarding our Sabbath practices come not just from friends and family; it is the plan of evil to assault anything that gives the heart true freedom and joy. There are times I have had to laugh at the blatantly obvious ways the evil one has tried to compromise the day. The best way to protect the Sabbath is to make well-anticipated plans. The next is to avoid realms that are obvious conduits of distressing or demanding news, such as e-mail, voice mail, even phone calls. Routine tasks, like checking mail, doing laundry, or stopping at a convenience store, often have a way of snowballing into more activity and a turning from the bride.

> *The best way to protect the Sabbath is*
> *to make well-anticipated plans.*

Almost every book on the Sabbath says, "Don't be legalistic." I couldn't agree more. Yet I know that evil works through subtle means to divert and eventually to destroy.

Over the course of many Sabbaths, you will begin to see where you need to be more diligent and wise. In the meantime, anticipate the large assaults, prepare adequate protection, and allow your heart to embrace the rhythms of eternity.

4

COMMUNAL FEAST

THE SABBATH IS A SENSUAL DELIGHT TO BE ENJOYED IN communion with God, others, and creation. It is a dance that moves to the rhythm of beauty, sensuality, and feasting. There is no notion more at odds with the Sabbath than a day of forced quiet, spiritual exercises, and religious devotion and attendance. It implies that the day is meant to be spent indoors, napping or praying, but not partying. Instead, the Sabbath is a day of sensuality when we say to one another, "Taste and see that the LORD is good. Oh, the joys of those who take refuge in him!" (Ps. 34:8).

THE RELATIONAL BIND

There seem to be many who long not only for a day off, but to be free from the entanglements of relationship. Many mothers view the Sabbath as a setup that isolates them from their peers and care partners (school, day care, baby-sitting, peer play groups) and dumps them with inattentive husbands and cranky kids. For many husbands, the day is at best a quiet day of reading and watching sports mixed with church and a few down moments before the hectic new workweek starts. It seems like the only way to make the day meaningful is to exhaust oneself with plans and activities that seem to ruin the Sabbath.

> *The Sabbath is a day of sensuality when we say to one another, "Taste and see that the Lord is good."*

The bind is if one lets the day happen spontaneously, it will usually dissolve into the route of least resistance, often turning out to be what Eugene Peterson refers to as a "bastard Sabbath."[1] If you make plans and work to execute them, it requires energy, planning, and intentionality—which often feel exhausting when what you want is time off from those same requirements that are required in droves during the rest of the week.

The bind is only resolvable with clarity as to why the Sabbath is about relationship, nature, and beauty. And even then, it still requires a strong push to embrace beauty.

TRINITY, ECOLOGY, AND AESTHETICS

If the Sabbath sends us anywhere, it is to nature. To spend the day entirely inside on the Sabbath is to forget the sounds of bird twill, the rush of the wind, and the warming fragrance of the dawn. It is to forget God even if we are indoors thinking about him. We must enter the earth to be struck dumb by the beauty of the Trinity. Our task is to plan to be near the face of God, in his creation, and then allow our plans to take shape as we are made alive by the surprise of his world.

Jürgan Mottman writes, "The true meaning of Sabbath is ecological. Related to it is also an esthetic aspect: Only someone who comes to rest and has nothing planned is able to perceive the beauty of things. He or she sees the flowers and the sunset, a painting or a vase or a beloved person with unintentional/unexpected pleasure."[2]

Moltmann invites us to the stunning simplicity of learning to see again. The agenda-ridden, task-driven focus that we use the other six days needs to be put to rest in order to receive the surprising bounty of the unexpected. We must plan to enter the realm where plans no longer hold sway.

Karl Barth writes about the Trinity and beauty. He says, "God's triune being 'is radiant, and what it radiates is joy. It attracts and therefore it conquers. It is, therefore, beautiful.' In other words, the triunity of God, its difference in unity, its relationality and harmony, its being and economy, its loving interweaving of persons (*perichoresis*) as if in a cosmic dance, radiate beauty."[3] The Sabbath is a day when we enter a dance with God and others and experience a beauty that takes our breath away.

> *The Sabbath is a day when we enter a dance with God and others and experience a beauty that takes our breath away.*

This dance is communal with God because he is three persons—a unity of being and becoming that has existed as the Godhead for eternity. And this triune God calls us not only to dance with him, but to dance with others in celebration of his beauty. The Trinity joins us with all others, including the earth itself, in a relationship that is based on the commonality of being made in the image of God. We are bound to one another, and we are called to adore and honor the earth as God's art, especially on the day that God has set aside to marvel at his own creation.

To enter the joy of the Sabbath, we will look at a theology of beauty, sensuality, and feasting.

BEAUTY

Beauty is in the eye of the beholder. Beauty is a given that reflects a form created by God. Which sentence strikes you as more true? The first sentence reflects an assumption that our take on beauty is highly individualistic and subjective. This is the most common view of beauty—it is subjectively constructed by each individual.

However, studies have shown that what we consider a beautiful face has consistency between people and cultures.[4] A beautiful face involves a relationship between harmony and distinctiveness. The greater harmony between the left and right side of the face, the greater our appreciation, but near perfect symmetry is not enough. Beauty does have unity or order, but it also has to be distinct or uncommon.

True beauty reflects both the unity and diversity of the Trinity. The Father, Son, and Holy Spirit are equal, alike in their being yet utterly different in their person. We want unity, but unity alone becomes dull; we long for diversity, yet diversity without union is chaos. We hate both boredom and chaos; we were made to long for union and uniqueness because we were created for a relationship with our trinitarian God.

There is significant variance in what we each find to be beautiful, yet all beauty is a play between the one and the many; harmony and diversity bring both a sense of union and awe. What is beauty? David Bentley Hart reminds us that "beauty indicates nothing: neither exactly a quality, nor a property, nor a function, not even really a subjective reaction to an object or occurrence. . . . Yet nothing else impresses itself upon our attention with at once so wonderful a power and so evocative an immediacy."[5] Beauty is not under our control and mastery—we cannot easily define it and own it. But when we encounter it, we are its servant.

The form of beauty created by God that most reveals what is beautiful is the person of Jesus Christ and his life, death, resurrection, and ascension. According to Karl Barth and Hans

Urs von Balthasar, "God's beauty is God's power to attract, to give pleasure, to create desire, to awaken joy and wonder."[6]

What most awakens desire, joy, and wonder for a Christian? Nothing in creation opens the heart to the presence of beauty like the incarnation. God became flesh; Jesus is both fully God and fully human. It is beyond our grasp; yet the incarnation throws us into wonder and delight in a manner similar to all lesser beauty.

The incarnation cannot be grasped or explained; it is utterly beyond what our experience can comprehend. Yet it can be enjoyed due to the extravagance and opulence of the gift of God's Son on our behalf. For God to become human means that humanity is brimming with the full presence of God, and God has taken into the Trinity the fullness of humanity. Jesus, the fullness of God and man, is the full perfection of humanity, and he calls us to a humanity that is full and alive, without flaw or fault. Jesus is unique and generously opulent.

We can approach beauty only through awe. Awe enables us to be both humbled and bold. Artists I have spoken to tell me that when an idea comes for a painting, a play, or a song, there is a sense of receiving something that is not theirs, yet is entrusted to them and demands engagement. As the idea begins to form, there is excitement, sometimes struggle, but always a sense of something beckoning to a more robust and compelling creation. In the moment of labor's completion, there is the exhaustion and exhilaration of gazing at the masterpiece that is and isn't one's own creation.

We can approach beauty only through awe.

An orthopedic surgeon once described the process of creating a solution to a broken body that could not be bound together by normal means. He left the operating room and sat in an adjacent room, imagining ways a clamp he had rarely used might be reconceived to do something it had not been created to do. He returned and began a creation he had never tried and that demanded more than he had the prior skill to do. It succeeded. He said, "It was beautiful. I knew I had created something the original maker had no idea of doing, yet I followed a path given to me that felt like a generous gift." How could it be both? How could Jesus be both fully human and fully God? The incarnation gives us a window into mystery that prompts us to see all of life differently, even if we comprehend little of what we see.

As I wrote this chapter, my eyes were taken from my task by hundreds of swallows that raced by my window in a derby. They flew in one direction at breakneck speeds en masse—and as suddenly turned midair and circled back racing for their lives in a ballet of flutter and flight that made me wonder and laugh. I looked out the window for at least ten minutes and forgot that I was writing. When I reread what I had written, I couldn't help but laugh again. How odd. How kind. I was given a 3-D illustration of my flat, two-dimensional words.

Jonathan Edwards, the Puritan theologian of the eighteenth century, was one of the first Protestant theologians of beauty. He stressed that nature functioned like a school of desire that awakens in us a hunger for beauty. "Edwards continually sought to integrate mind and heart in the apprehension of both God's beauty and the earth's wonder. Divine grace allows us to see the world in all its mystery, and, in turn, the world of senses trains our perception in glimpsing God's grandeur. . . . This is a knowing that involves a tasting and delighting—not just an apprehension of the mind, but an intimate engagement of all the senses as well."[7]

God intends the beauty in nature to arouse us and to capture our hearts to desire him. This requires opening our senses to beauty.

SENSUALITY

The Sabbath is intended to be the most sensual day of the week. For many, the thought of a sensuous day is at best slated as Valentine's Day. Or as sensuality enters the realm of religion, it is viewed as the feast of celebration before a period of Lent, which we normally call Mardi Gras. It is not weekly, and certainly not spiritual.

Sabbath is meant to be a dalliance with senses because we are called not to move too fast, or too far, or focus on the normal features of daily functioning. It is a riot of senses, a celebration of smell, touch, hearing, seeing, and especially taste. We can't be caught up with the otherness and opulence of beauty without sensual connection to our world. Diane Ackerman writes, "The senses don't just *make sense* of life in bold or subtle acts of clarity, they tear reality apart into vibrant morsels and reassemble them into a meaningful pattern . . . the senses feed shards of information to the brain like microscopic pieces of a jigsaw puzzle. When enough 'pieces' assemble, the brain says *Cow. I see a cow.*"[8]

Due to many factors, we are trained to be highly suspicious of our senses. There is no formal part of our education that is intended to grow our capacities to sense. A quote from Augustine marks the dilemma:

But what do I love when I love my God? Not material beauty or beauty of a temporal order; not the brilliance of earthly light, so welcome to our eyes; not the sweet melody of harmony and song; not the fragrance of flowers, perfumes, and spices; not manna or honey; not limbs such as the body delights to embrace. It is not these that I love when I love my God. And yet, when I love him, it is true that I love a light of a certain kind, a voice, a perfume, a food, an embrace; but they are of the kind that I love in my inner self, when my soul is bathed in light that is not bound by space; when it listens to sound that never dies away; when it breathes fragrance that is not bourne away on the wind; when it tastes food that is never consumed by eating; when it clings to embrace from which it is not severed by fulfillment of desire. That is what I love when I love my God.[9]

Augustine is highly suspicious of our senses. They can easily take us from God and consume us or deceive us in thinking we have discovered God only to have found a trace, not the real presence. Augustine worked hard to escape any sense that seemed to press him to desire more; only God has the right to evoke more desire, not something sensual. Augustine said, "I used to be much more fascinated by the pleasures of sound than the pleasures of smell. I was enthralled by them, but you broke my bonds and set me free. I admit that I still find some enjoyment in the music of hymns, which are alive with your praises, when I hear them sung by well-trained, melodious voices. But I do not enjoy it so much that I cannot tear myself away."[10]

Which is worse: being highly attached to the arousal of our senses, or being so detached that nothing but megadoses of arousal even slightly awaken us? We live in a day when our senses are so dull that we need extreme sports, bingeing, or dangerous pastimes to give us a sense we are alive. We crave reality—both pain and pleasure—so much that many young people cut themselves, saying, "I just wanted to feel something." If Augustine was concerned about the dark potential for sense experience to take us away from God, then in our day, it is no less a concern that so many live so detached from the gift of our senses.

Augustine warns us to be suspicious of our sensuality; the theologian Julian invites us to celebrate our senses. She writes, "God is nearer to us than to our own soul, because God is the ground in which our soul stands and God is the means whereby our Substance and our Sensuality are kept together so as to never be apart."[11] She encloses God in our sensuality without losing the distinctiveness and eternality of God in our being. She speaks of mystery and sense with far greater generosity than the suspicious side-glance of Augustine.

Whereas Augustine situates the nature of reality in two cities—the city of God and the city of man, which are always at war and never at peace—Julian writes, "Our Sensuality is the beautiful City in which our Lord Jesus sits and in which He is enclosed."[12] It would be grand to simply choose which perspective fits you better than the other—if you are a sexual addict like Augustine, then suspicion of our senses seems reasonable; if you are more at ease in your body, then Julian's acceptance of sensuality may fit better. The truth, like all matters of theology, likely resides in the unsayable, the not fully communicable middle that makes the writer (in this case, me) look like a thoughtless compromiser, a sloppy-thinking ne'er-do-well.

Yet read the sensuous and womb-honoring writing of Diane Ackerman: "But for a baby in the womb the mother's heartbeat performs the ultimate cradlesong of peace and plenty; the surflike waves of her respiration lull and soothe. The womb is a snug, familiar landscape, an envelope of rhythmic warmth, and the mother's heartbeat a steady clarion of safety."[13]

I don't recall being in the womb, but I have never considered the peace of that home as deeply and richly until I read her sea-rhythm, heart-cadence, warm-lullaby words. I am mesmerized by the question: "Is that what I felt?" I cannot know, but I can say that I want what Ackerman pens to be an experience of being so near to God that I can hear the cradlesong of God's heart, the lapping resonance of her breathing, and the holding ground of her skin surrounding me in divine safety and warmth. To disparage sensuousness is to stand at arm's length from the incarnation, allowing it to be objective and abstract. The Sabbath is the context for our senses to be unfettered and unattached from the oily grind of the soiled world of work.

FEASTING

My wife and I hurried home for the start of the Sabbath. We had done our shopping and had lunch in a pub by an inlet of Puget Sound. The February day was warmer than usual, and we had walked a fair distance to sample the smells of the harbor. Sea air is briny and fresh. It is as if the sky has allowed the seasoning of the sea to give a dash of salt to the evergreen-laden air. We strolled by Andante Coffee with interest since many friends nuzzle into the soft chairs to read. We were with two other couples— dear friends from Vancouver, British Columbia, who had joined us for the weekend. They were willing to participate in Sabbath, but we had talked little about what our time would bring.

We went into a music store and I asked them each to pick up a CD that reminded them of some significant part of their adolescence. The shopping took far longer because it was not an easy exercise. They were intrigued and wanted to know why. I simply told them Sabbath was coming in a few hours, and there are many mysteries associated with a day of delight.

My wife had prepared a sumptuous meal garnished with many colors of vegetables, freshly baked bread, oils, and olives. Tantalizing aromas swirled from the soup, and the salad was crisp and delicately covered with homemade dressing. I helped, but I am a better deliverer of food than a chef. We played some of the music, talked and ate; we cleaned our dishes together and then sat down for an excellent array of fragrances, music, drink, and stories.

Some of us smoked pipes, and the various hues of tobacco filled the air. We poured rich and well-apportioned coffees, teas, and drinks. We were too full to start dessert, yet the night was young and the CDs were being looked at with intrigue. I asked if I could read a few of the pages of this book, and we talked about what Sabbath has been and how we each had either come to ignore it or break it with impunity. No one in our community of six had had long-lasting experiences of joy surrounding the Sabbath.

After some conversation, I asked the group to pick one or two songs from the CD they chose and to tell some of the stories they associated with that song or artist. We know one another well enough to tell truly true stories, yet not so well that we knew what stories would be told. The night was magical. It was a feast of pleasure, of tears, laughter, and amazement at the odd and gracious ways God has stepped out of music to touch our lives. Few would consider the music we played to be spiritual, yet it was deeply wed to our flight from God and equally to our search for what only the heart can know in God.

It was a feast night, a party. I put my head on the pillow that night amazed that I got to be with Don and Katie, Peter and Debbie, and my wife. I was honored to hear stories that whet my appetite for the day I will join them feasting with Jesus. I long for the next time we will be with our Canadian friends on this earth. The delight of the Sabbath is not merely a gathering with good food and friends—there are many nights for such gatherings; but there is no one night that is so gloriously set aside for a taste of wonder that ushers us into the eternal party of God.

David Ford writes, "All the senses are engaged in a good feast. We taste, touch, smell, see, hear. Salvation as health is here vividly physical. Anything that heals and enhances savoring the world through our senses may feed into a salvation that culminates in feasting. . . . Jesus went to meals, weddings and parties and had a feast-centered ethic. . . . That combination of sharing and celebrating is, perhaps, the most radical of all the implications of the teaching and practice of Jesus."[14] Jesus is the presence of superabundance. The Sabbath is the weekly entry into a taste of lavish, sensuous delight.

One Sabbath night in Ethiopia, my wife and I had the privilege of being at the home of our translator, Wonde. Wonde's wife had soaked the lamb in spices for several days. The home had been cleaned and prepared for us as if we were royalty. I will never forget those first few moments of the family's delight when we entered their home. As the door opened, the children's faces were wild with curiosity, and they clamored to get a look at their strange visitors. We were enveloped in their care and the fragrance of the meal we were about to eat. It was abundantly clear that we were eating an extravagant meal that may have cost what the family would spend on food in a month.

The sacrifice of the family was part of their joy; there was no way to reciprocate other than to join in their joy and to add to their immense sacrifice, our humble gratitude in being so undeservedly blessed. Jesus' way of being with others was a feast ethic. All meals, and all joy around a table, are a reminder of the feast of the coming kingdom. We are to eat and anticipate the day of plenty in which we will dine with Jesus at the head of the table.

That night, we ate with Wonde and Tsirit and their children. We did not talk about eschatology or the meal we will partake in the kingdom of God, nor did we have the Lord's Table, as the Eucharist. But in a way we did, because we feasted in the joy of the Lord.

What if the Sabbath is creating space to hear the Father speak to us as his beloved as he serves us as the Host?

As we enjoyed our meal together, we heard stories about each of Wonde's children. And when their father told of their feats of bravery, wisdom, and kindness, they beamed. I had never seen a father so proud and so free to glory in his children. I basked in their smiles.

I could not keep from wondering what it would be like to have a father speak about me with such joy. What if the Sabbath is creating space to hear the Father speak to us as his beloved as he serves us as the Host? This day is ours, given to us by the Trinity for our entry into the wild wonder of Jesus' love for us.

5

PLAY DAY

IN GOD'S ECONOMY, THERE IS NO DISTINCTION BETWEEN work and play; his creation is not due to lack, loneliness, or necessity. It was free and groundless—that is, without reason, other than delight. As Jürgen Moltmann writes,

> Faith answers the unchildish childhood question in a childlike way; and the wisdom of theology ends with the liberty of the children of God. There is no purposive rationale for the proposition that something exists rather than nothing. The existence of the world is not necessary . . . When [God] creates something that is not god but also not nothing, then this must have its ground not in itself but in God's *good will or pleasure*. Hence the creation is God's play, a play of his groundless and inscrutable wisdom. It is the realm in which God displays his glory.[1]

The reason of creation is God—which is no explanation, yet it offers a radical beginning point to consider how we are to live out our Sabbath, the day that most defines how we are to live our lives.

The Sabbath is our play day—not as a break from the routine of work, but as a feast that celebrates the superabundance of God's creative love to give glory for no other reason other than Love himself loves to create and give away glory. Inherent in this discussion is the distinction between work and play.

Most see the day as a chance to rest—to be off, away from work. In this view, it is as if the six days of creation were hard, onerous work for God that required a rest day for him to recuperate, in order to get back to the work of waiting for Adam and Eve to sin, in order to get the other part of the plan of redemption off the ground. What a busy God!

We too easily allow ourselves to see God, and especially the Sabbath, with human-bound categories that make God an idol made in our image, rather than allowing God to form us and reshape us in his image. Sabbath is not a break from work; it is a redefinition of how we work, why we work, and how we create freedom through our work.

> *Sabbath is not a break from work; it is a*
> *redefinition of how we work, why we work,*
> *and how we create freedom through our work.*

We are told in the first giving of the Law, Exodus 20, to remember the Sabbath through the lens of creation. In the second giving of the Law, we are told to observe the Sabbath and to remember the Exodus from Egypt as the reason for keeping the day holy:

Observe the Sabbath day by keeping it holy, as the LORD your God has commanded you. You have six days each week for your ordinary work, but the seventh day is a Sabbath day of rest dedicated to the LORD your God. On that day no one in your household may do any work. This includes you, your sons and daughters, your male and female servants, your oxen and donkeys and other livestock, and any foreigners living among you. All your male and female servants must rest as you do. Remember that you were once slaves in Egypt, but the LORD your God brought you out with his strong hand and powerful arm. That is why the LORD your God has commanded you to rest on the Sabbath day. (Deut. 5:12–15)

Sabbath is celebrated because redemption (the Exodus) *created* a new people who would fulfill God's promise to Abraham to bless the earth and all its people. Sabbath is about the blessing of creativity, the making of something new that is full of surprise and glory that will bless through the lavish, free, and playful kindness of God. For that reason, one cannot understand Sabbath unless the concept of play is given a strong and compelling voice.

LIBERATING PLAY

Play is a category that has not often been engaged in academic theological circles. I suspect this is because, like studying humor, nothing seems more incongruent than ruining something by studying it. How does one study play, playfully? For many, play is either regarded as a long-lost childhood experience or as something that seldom was experienced even as children. It seems few of us know how to play. If we are to learn, it is primarily by watching and imitating children.

If you have the opportunity, go watch your children or any children play. Notice that in any childhood game there are rules, but they morph and change. Often there is tension or conflict, but it gets worked through the process of creating new ways of playing the game or relating to the other children and the toys in the game. If one player is better, a handicap may be imposed to make the game more equal; yet the goal, even if the supposed end point is winning, is to intensify pleasure by trying out new ways of doing the game that honor the routine yet risk what has not yet been tried.

If that is unclear, then go snorkeling in the Caribbean and notice the arrangement of diversity of color, shape, size, and movement of something as simple as fish. God's love of variety is on parade around every reef. It is as if God splashed color over a canvas and then stretched the canvas to see what would happen to the image when color and shape are bent in new ways. Jürgen Moltmann, a theologian whose work centers on the interplay of creation, liberation, future, and play, writes,

> We enjoy freedom when we anticipate by playing what can and shall be different and when in the process we break the bonds of the immutable status quo . . . the significance of games is identical with that of the arts, namely to construct 'anti-environments' and 'counter-environments' to ordinary and everyday human environments and through the conscious confrontation of these to open up creative freedom and future alternatives. We are no longer playing merely with the past in order to escape it for a while, but we are increasingly playing with the future in order to get to know it."[2]

Even in the nonhuman kingdom, play is part of the creational mandate. Diane Ackerman says, "The more an animal needs to learn in order to survive, the more it needs to play."[3] Our capacity to adapt requires us to learn the past and then unhinge it to open up the possibility of a new future. The core of all play is linking what is known (past) to what is yet to be created (future) with the freedom to risk, to fail, and to recreate. This is true whether we are playing a pickup game of hoops or starting a new seminary.

The Sabbath creates equality between male and female, slave and free, alien and aristocracy because we all were once slaves and have been set free by the recreational goodness of

God. This may be one of the reasons we are so averse to play and prefer the tedium of work—freedom scares us. We demand freedom, yet we fear the risk required to recreate in a manner that has such openness, vulnerability, and potential for failure.

RISKY PLAY

In her book *Deep Play*, Diane Ackerman playfully writes about the origins of our word *play*. She says, "In Indo-European, *plegan* (the word for play) meant to risk, chance, expose oneself to hazard. A *pledge* was integral to the act of play, as was danger (cognate words are *peril* and *plight*). Play's original purpose was to make a pledge to someone or something by risking one's life."[4] If one can't lose, then it is not play.

Play redistributes power and gives the opportunity for convention to be reconfigured by the unexpected and the inconceivable. Almost every sports movie plays the story of the underdog against the expected winners; an upset is more savory and desired than the predictable winner being reenthroned.

The tried-and-true expect to win. Usually the favored team is arrogant and self-satisfied in their victories and dismissive of their opponent. As a moviegoing audience, we can't stand smug winners. On the other hand, we love underdogs. The underdog invites us to rail against the oppressive regime that we have grown accustomed to serving and have compromised ourselves to gain.

Yet as much as we love the underdog, we don't want to be one. We'd rather be the fat, privileged, and powerful; yet we justify our struggle by seeing ourselves as equally disenfranchised. It is a no-win situation, so we project our ambivalence to a team or a contest rather than facing the contradiction in our own situation.

Imagine a friend asked you, "What do you most want to be, to do, to know, and to give away in the last third of your life?" How would you respond? Many of us would be irritated. We don't know. We don't have time to ponder the question. To be honest, I don't really want to be asked such an impossible question—we feel overwhelmed because we have kids to support and a house to pay off, and tonight our favorite reality TV show is on and we'd rather watch people lose weight than do the same. The weight of life, sometimes, makes it easier to escape personal risk and to enter vicariously the risks of others.

Play is not diversion, if it is truly risky. Instead, it is the highest call to plunge into the unknown and to commit to a course of action that may bring more suffering than remaining ensconced on the couch. I want the tidy and true; I crave the wild and unknown.

If the Sabbath is the height of play, then the distance to fall will be immense. There is meant to be more risk and danger on the Sabbath than any other day. It is the risk of playing with God communally amid his creation, aroused by sensuality, and open to the terrifying presence of the Trinity.

There is meant to be more risk and danger
on the Sabbath than any other day.

GOD PLAY

When I asked my Sabbath class what they perceived they should be doing on the Sabbath, the most tragic and consistent response was "being quiet, reading the Bible, praying, and thinking about God." In one sense, it is so close to the truth it is heresy. Heresy is so dangerous not because it is ridiculously false, but because it is deceptively almost true. Playing with God is a risky spin of Russian roulette where we gamble on a bet that may cost us our lives. C. S. Lewis captured this well when he wrote, "There comes a moment when the children who have been playing at burglars hush suddenly: was that a *real* footstep in the hall? There comes a moment when people who have been dabbling in religion . . . suddenly draw back. Supposing we really found Him? We never meant to come to *that!* Worse still, supposing He had found us?"[5]

Belden Lane offers a terrifying and thrilling proposition: perhaps God is truly playful. When we experience God's absence, perhaps God is "like a mother playfully hiding from her child or a lover playing hard to get, God hides from those God loves, occasionally playing rough for love's sake. The purpose of God's apparent absence, of God's hiding, is to deepen in the lover a longing for the one loved, to enhance the joy experienced when fear dissolves and the separated are rejoined."[6]

It is disturbing enough to cast God out of the garden. It conjures our deepest fear, as C. S. Lewis spoke about, being the toy in a divine game that is cruel and vile. Yet what do we do with the book of Job? Satan strolls into God's presence with a gamble that God takes as a worthy contest. Even as a literary convention, it is radically disturbing to our sensibilities. No wonder we don't like play, especially when it has to do with faith. Instead, we want the tried-and-true, the established and fundamentally solid. It is just too much freedom and risk to play with God.

Lane argues that our play with God requires us to be wakeful and simultaneously disengaged.[7] It is the mystery of all deep play. To enter the realm of play, we must give ourselves to something or someone and turn away from all else. It is both a pledge and a betrayal.

Think about what is required to hit a good return of serve in a tennis match. I must attend to the stance of my playmate. As he throws the ball into the air, I look for any indication he is going to hit wide or go down the middle. I must be moving into the ball, ready, available, not yet making a commitment but prepared to do so in an instant. As I see the ball twist toward the corner, I not only have to move rapidly to my right, but I need to take into account that the ball will rapidly spin to the right the moment it touches the ground. I must turn from all the other distractions around me—the sound of the kids whacking stones outside the gate, the creak in my knee as I bend to the right—in order to hit the forehand shot down the right line, since I also noted my friend is coming to the net to score an easy point.

If I am aware of thinking any of these thoughts in the process, then it is unlikely I will even touch the ball. I must do so instinctively after countless encounters of failure. Playing is failing—at least failing so many times that we succeed only by the gift of grit and desire that is the real point of all play. To endure and to grow in desire is why God our mother hides and waits for our fear to rise.

> *Playing is failing—at least failing so many times that we succeed only by the gift of grit and desire that is the real point of all play.*

We hide and desperately hope to be found. Our good mother knows when to return quickly when our fear is beyond our capacity to endure the anxiety of her absence. She also knows when her departure is necessary to sustain even when our fear rises beyond the heavens. God knows our frailty and our courage and never confuses one for the other and knows how to comfort and call forth when we would prefer God to simply answer us as we desire. More than any other purpose, God plays for the victory of union. We seek and hope to be reunited.

All play is the desire not for victory but reunion, for a coalescence of those divided to be reunited, and to celebrate. It requires not only immense focus but great loss. I can't focus unless I choose not to attend to many other matters that are in and of themselves equally deserving of my attention.

How can I write unless I read? How can I take time to read when so many other compelling demands call out for my engagement? Yet as I focus on words in a book or, with my camera, a bird in the tree, how do I know that I will capture the moment as I hope? Even in attending, I risk because I have to wait. I have to sit and read and wait. The more I push for meaning, the more calcified the sentence reads. The more I angle for a better shot of the plumage, the more likely I will spring the preening eagle from its nest and lose the shot I have so diligently waited to capture.

If I move, I fail. If I sit, I am blocked by the branch. The nature of play is that it exposes our demand for mastery as fleeting and illusionary. Our deeper hunger for mystery requires us to move and wait and to be thrilled when the moment comes that we are captured by the words we have written or the picture we have taken—because we had a part, yet only a small part in the play.

REGENERATIVE PLAY

I have fly-fished for well over a decade because I needed the solace of kind of play other than being part of a start-up graduate school. I know at the depths of my being that I would never have survived the heartache and broken hopes of a start-up unless I had the gift of this game.

One of my sweetest moments happened in the first several years of fly-fishing. One of my mentors and I were fishing a portion of the Frying Pan River near Aspen, Colorado. The river had turned a quiet bend and then began a section that ran downhill. The water was flowing too rapidly to fish, so we walked on the road until we could come to a flat section. He had a biological necessity to address, so I stood looking at a moderate-sized boulder in the middle of the rapids. I noticed there was a small flat section of water right behind the boulder. I had a few minutes to waste and thought I'd practice trying to put my fly on the flat water. I had no more thought of catching a fish than being elected president.

I unstrung my rod and dabbed a small slick of solution on the fly to make it float with greater ease. I laughed at myself performing the task as if I could get it into the small area or as if a fish would rise in that fast water to snag my fly. My first cast hit the flat with precision, and the water exploded. My fly was consumed by a fish that sucked down the fly as it ascended out of the water in my full view. The fish rose with such tenacity that at one point I felt like it was going to fly away with my fly, line, rod, and reel. I didn't know what to do. I had never dealt with an airborne fish. Somehow it hit the water and thus began a fifteen-minute ordeal that included falling down a small waterfall.

My mentor returned to watch the display unfold. He was as stunned as I and far, far more delighted than I had the capacity to feel in the moment. The joy on his face was more captivating than the glory in the water. It took many years for me to comprehend, but the first fish my father-in-law caught on a small stream in Montana was as exciting to me as any fish I have ever caught. I recall far better the fish my son caught last summer after we nearly fell down a twenty-foot cliff into the water. I have come close to drowning several times, suffered hypothermia in New Zealand, and walked through grizzly country, but nothing has been as moving for me as being part of another person's joy.

The deepest delight is to participate with another in a delight that we have had a small hand in bringing to pass. To create opportunity for another to know joy is regenerating both for the giver and for the one who receives, and the combined joy is a gift we return to the Creator for offering us such bounty in his creation.

A friend who is a split-bamboo-rod maker extraordinaire told me once of a famous rod maker who refused to share any of his secrets with younger rod makers. His cane work was impeccable and fetched huge sums of money. He held on to his art with cantankerous spite. But when a rod would break, no one knew how to fix it since the rod maker's technique was undisclosed. As a result, his rods lost value, and over time few purchased his goods. My friend, on the other hand, offers workshops to teach novices his art. My friend loves to see people shine. Regeneration requires giving away for new growth to spring forth. It is the Sabbath way.

SABBATH PLAY

Sabbath calls forth play together in the sensual beauty of God's creation, in order to taste and see God's delight. Abraham Heschel warns us that the Sabbath is "not a day to shoot fireworks or to turn somersaults, but an opportunity to mend our tattered lives; to collect rather than to dissipate time."[8] We can come near the Sabbath by merely stopping the oppressive routine of our workweek and spending the time in congenial and gentle rest. It is good, but not all the Sabbath is meant to be. But how will we know until we fashion a Sabbath and find it adequate, but not as full as we long for it to be?

We must be willing to fail at Sabbath to learn to play well. One friend, a single woman, invited friends over to her apartment for the beginning of Sabbath. She had created an interactive game that required each team to discover things about each other. Two teams were chosen, and each team was sent to a separate room. Everyone was to share an embarrassing story, and then the team was to weave each incident into a single story that was plausible.

We must be willing to fail at Sabbath to learn to play well.

It turned into a fiasco. Some refused to share; others refused to develop a story. One person said, "When you said we were going to have a Sabbath together, I thought we were going to pray, instead, we did a stupid icebreaker." Creativity risks being foolish—to do the tried-and-true is to repeat convention with no possibility of shame. No wonder we'd rather subject ourselves to a restful day off than risk true play.

If we aspire to a more life-giving delight, then we will need to go further into the heart of the Sabbath. It is a simple principle: we get of God what we desire. The more we desire, the wilder the journey becomes. If we are satisfied with only a little rest, then the full inheritance of the day will await our desire to propel us further than we have come.

Imagine a Sabbath spent as a walk in the woods with a dear friend. It may be a quiet walk in the presence of someone who doesn't need idle words to fill the space. Or it might be a rambling conversation that bubbles up like an underground stream. If the walk is with someone who acknowledges the sensual holiness of the day, then at any moment God might break into the conversation, or he might remain hidden, not yet to be found.

I recall one such Sabbath. It was an early spring afternoon, and the day was brimming with the first splashes of warmth. I was walking with a friend from seminary in a Philadelphia city park. My friend recited a portion of a T. S. Elliott poem from memory:

April is the cruelest month, breeding
Lilacs out of the dead, land mixing
Memory and desire, stirring
Dull roots with spring rain.
Winter kept us warm, covering
Earth in forgetful snow, feeding
A little life with dried tubers.[9]

I asked why he had put this verse to memory. Over two hours we talked of April's cruelty, the comfort of winter's death, and the terror of awakening unbidden desire. It was the first time I spoke to him about my father's death and the possibility that his shadow remains. Though the conversation occurred thirty-three years ago, I can still remember that long, slow walk. And yesterday, on our Sabbath walk, my wife and I reentered the spring cruelty on the second anniversary of her father's death. Our hearts were filled with a fierce hunger for a father we never had and will never know. On this cloudy, rain-filled walk, we stopped on a lichen-covered fallen tree and asked our Father to come play.

After sitting for an interminable wait in the rain, God did not arrive. We were about to leave when Becky looked up and pointed to my right. On a tree about forty yards away sat an owl, a regal Solomon surveying his realm. He took flight, and his wide expanse momentarily filled the sky. Coincidence? A sign from God? A random act of nature? I don't know. I simply delighted in the random gift my Father offered amid April cruelty.

To play in the fields of God will vary from Sabbath to Sabbath. There will be countless Sabbaths spent indoors in front of a fire, reading a novel; and there will be others on the side of a stream watching a bull trout meander with feckless disregard as fleeing cutthroat escape their most potent rival. But all Sabbaths are a direct, face-to-face, underdog challenger to death. The Sabbath looks death in the eye and says, "O death, where is your sting?" (1 Cor. 15:55).

Sabbath doesn't deny that death exists; instead, it celebrates life.

Sabbath doesn't deny that death exists; instead, it celebrates life. It pretends that death has no power to contort joy or to disfigure love. It risks the foolishness of childlike faith to overcome the bully that seeks at every moment to ruin play and malign joy. As we will discover in part 2, Sabbath is God's re-creation of division as shalom, destitution as abundance, and death as joy.

PART 2

SABBATH PURPOSE

6

SABBATH PLAY: DIVISION SURRENDERS TO SHALOM

I FINISHED EIGHT HOURS OF COUNSELING OVER FOUR days with a young pastor whose wife has chosen to divorce him. The young man has been thrown into a nightmare of heartache that is not uncommon in our litigious, divorce-glutted culture. As one of a number of spiritual resources who had earlier worked with this couple to help them reflect on their struggles, I had hope, great hope, that they would thrive. Yet he returned alone, after she had chosen to divorce, to address the question: "How am I to live now with this heartache and the call God has on me?"

I recall the same question posed to me when I was his age, just starting to counsel, by an older man who asked, "How am I to go to the party God offers, when the one woman on earth I love has chosen not to attend with me?" I had little to offer, now or then, beyond the deep respect that the question was asked of me. The wise, godly older man's question has haunted me for twenty-five years. I can still see his tears and the lines of exhaustion in his face. I can still feel the youthful urge to give him mitigating words of hope, and I am grateful, beyond words, that I offered few words at all. How do we go to the party when we have known such loss?

DIVISION AND THE CONQUERING OF EVIL

Divide and conquer—it is the rule of all military operations. Let your enemy get ahead of their supply lines, and then flank them to disrupt the flow of food and armaments. Isolate. Create diversion, bait arrogant hope, and then scatter the order with cruel division. If you are living in any manner that is a threat to the kingdom of darkness, then you are under assault. Nothing wears our hearts down faster or deeper than division in our closest and dearest relationships.

> *Nothing wears our hearts down faster or deeper*
> *than division in our closest and dearest relationships.*

David cries out in Psalm 55, "It is not an enemy who taunts me—I could bear that. It is not my foes who so arrogantly insult me—I could have hidden from them. Instead, it is you—

my equal, my companion and close friend. What good fellowship we enjoyed as we walked together to the house of God"
(vv. 12–14). The lament stings from thousands of years ago.
The faces of those I grieve hover as I write. And I know those
whom I remember as my betrayers also sing the same song and
remember me.

We are divided, and the day of reconciliation seems farther
away than the bright moon that still shines in the early morning sky. Division always enlists, forms, and feeds new communities. Division breeds new alliances that provide us with the
ability to survive the heartache. We tell our story to a friend
who suffers the injustice with us. This friend sides with us to
some degree, and as a result he judges the one who brought the
pain. The new alliance spills out to others through gossip, and
deeper fissures are created in relationships much the same way
that an earthquake tears a landscape to bits.

We forget, quickly, that all division is more than two-sided;
it is complex, messy, and seldom involves the clarity that legal
or blog-spin analysts offer. We embrace the inevitability of the
division, especially when any move of reconciliation might dis-
turb the peace of our new relationships by exposing our failure.
It is easier to live with self-righteous indifference or thinly veiled
vengeance.

What is distributed into the air is the refuse of accusation.
Divisions always lead to disinformation that serves to sustain
our just right to see ourselves as the victim, the righteous one.

We vilify any good, jaundice every motive, and suspect each move of our enemy.

Accusation is the tool of evil that deepens every division. It is the power of all labeling, such as, "My ex-husband is a money-grubbing manipulator." "My boss is a coward who wouldn't know how to make a decision if it hit him in the face." "My son is a slacker." "My pastor is a self-righteous prig." "My neighbor is a narcissist." Accusations are totalizing, deprecating, and self-satisfying war cries that demand our allegiance to sustain our reserve of vitriol. It is like smoking cigarettes—cool, addictive, and self-soothing. Yet no one questions that it will destroy. The bitter tar of accusations will, over time, be the residue that steals, kills, and destroys beauty. The lungs were not meant to suffer such an infusion of darkness.

The evil one joins the accusations to spread more cancer. Yet evil works as quickly to turn the accusations against the one who accuses. Every time I have taken in that smoke and felt justified, I have heard, eventually, the words turned against me: "You are the loser. You don't have anything in you that loves God. You deserve all you are suffering, and it will get worse." It is diabolic.

If I turn up the accusations against my betrayer, I feel momentary relief, but at the price of harsher judgment that I know is not true. Yet it has to be true to keep a sense of relief. The flight from the more complex truth requires hardness and bitterness. The disease requires more disease for relief. I get sicker.

If I give up the accusations against my enemy, then I am susceptible to my accusatory voice, amplified by the voice of evil, and joined by those who oppose me. It is a dead end, a vicious bind that seems to have no way out. If this is true of individuals, then it is equally true for all systems that utilize labeling, accusations, and contempt to dehumanize their enemies, whether the enemy is a rival corporation or a nation-state. The structure of accusation and contempt and the binding of cobelligerents together on the basis of gossip and acrimony is how we keep denominations, tribal alliances, and political parties together.

To the degree this is accurate with those who break our hearts, then it can be assumed there is some truth to it with anyone who does less severe harm. Division exists in all relationships—in the happiest marriage, with children who are cutting a different path from their parents, and with friends who don't fully enter our joy or suffering as we wish. As I was writing, my wife called up to my study to help her with packing a car full of cardboard boxes for the dump. We had agreed I'd write undisturbed for another two hours. Her call for help grated against my Sabbath thoughts. I cringed and then went to help her, though with irritation.

After I aided her labor, I said, "Well, do I get an extra half hour since you interrupted my work?" She bristled, and we divided to our different enterprises. I had some unsavory thoughts about her need for order and her insouciant disregard of my work. I don't know what she thought about me, but I doubt it was charitable. The period of division was short, because I had just written about the process. But I only got up to confess to her and apologize after I had started to hear the echo of past accusations leveled against me by my enemy. It seemed too absurd to continue the darkness of accusation in the space of division when a mere word, in this case, needed to be uttered to reconcile us.

Sabbath is not a diversion; it is a radical entry into shalom.

Division in relationships is inevitable in a divided world, as divided people who are at odds with our own deepest desires. This is the reality that we wish to escape through our pain-lessening diversions. Sabbath is not a diversion; it is a radical entry into shalom.

SABBATH: THE FATHER'S WELCOME

The Sabbath is the day in which we receive and extend the Father's invitation to be reconciled. He welcomes us home and extends his arms to any who wish to know peace. It is the day we celebrate the newness of life, created, redeemed, restored, and set free. The apostle Paul uses wild language to describe the nature of our new condition and our calling. He writes,

> He died for everyone so that those who receive his new life will no longer live for themselves. Instead, they will live for Christ, who died and was raised for them.

So we have stopped evaluating others from a human point of view. At one time we thought of Christ merely from a human point of view. How differently we know him now! This means that anyone who belongs to Christ has become a new person. The old life is gone; a new life has begun!

And all of this is a gift from God, who brought us back to himself through Christ. And God has given us this task of reconciling people to him. For God was in Christ, reconciling the world to himself, no longer counting people's sins against them. And he gave us this wonderful message of reconciliation. (2 Cor. 5:15–19)

The lens of reconciliation allows us to see each person who has betrayed us and all of our betrayal from a radically different point of view. If division increases on the basis of self-justifying accusation, then reconciliation grows on the basis of self-giving service that annuls our right to vengeance. God, who has the right to the greatest claim to injustice, abolished that claim in the sufferings of the Crucified One and then restored—that is, re-created—life through the resurrection.

The Father wishes to seat us before our enemies and feed us, to welcome us all to his care and lavish upon us the richest of his delights (Ps. 23). The feast of justice that God has prepared was paid not by the blood of the betrayer, but by the suffering of God. It is a new day, a day in which the new creation is celebrated in the song, "There is no condemnation for those who belong to Christ Jesus" (Rom. 8:1).

Sabbath is the day we put to rest all tension, strife, and fighting. It is a day we pretend that all is well, our enemies are not at war with us, and the peace we will one day enjoy for eternity, is an eternity that utters this day on our behalf. Abraham Heschel writes,

> It [Sabbath] is the state in which there is no strife and no fighting, no fear and no distrust. . . . The Seventh day is the armistice in man's cruel struggle for existence, a truce in all conflicts personal and social, peace between man and man, man and nature, peace within man . . . exodus from tension, the liberation of man from his own muddiness, the installation of man as a sovereign in the world of time.[1]

Here is the key: we will one day be seated with every enemy and celebrate the Crucified and Risen One with abandon and delight. How might this day, then be our opportunity to pretend righteously?

PRETENDING PEACE

Pretense is as common as twenty-second sound bites on the evening news. We pretend daily that we are happy, productive, or at least busy. We pretend that we are interested in conversations, when we are bored and irritated. Our pretense in these matters is not merely a flight from reality; it is an intentional (sometimes blindly unaware) refusal to be the truth.

There is another kind of pretending—the kind we associate with playing as children or acting a part or a role as an adult. As the president of Mars Hill Graduate School, I have a part to play, and it has taken years to understand what that role requires. I have learned I can't pop into an office and in the middle of a conversation suggest an alternative plan for a project without creating havoc. A simple suggestion sets off a series of trip wires that can create confusion for an employee or an entire organization. We all have roles and expectations from others in how we are to play our part, with significant consequences when we violate tacit rules.

We also pretend when we dream in action what is not yet validated by the final result. For example, I pretend that I know the end of a lecture, when all I have is an idea. I pretended when I announced we were going to create a graduate school that would bring a new synthesis to text, soul, and culture, not really knowing what each term meant, or what a synthesis would really look like. One cannot create without pretending.

Pretending is risking the status quo—turning from the past to create a new future, dreaming what has not yet been for the sake of an unseen glory. It is allowing the "not yet" to be more real than the "is." And what is the truth we believe about the new heavens and earth to come? I believe it will be a day of peace, plenty, and partying. In this chapter, we will address pretending only the promise of peace; in the following chapters, we will consider what it means to pretend abundance and joy.

Sabbath is a fiction, true and sure, the promise of peace. How should this form our Sabbath? Simply, a Sabbath of peace gives no time to any division, accusation, or dark loyalty to one side versus another, nor to look into any abyss between the divided sides. Sabbath is a day that celebrates the one and true day of reconciliation.

> *Sabbath is a day that celebrates the one*
> *and true day of reconciliation.*

The Sabbath asks, how would you live if there were no wars, enmity, battle lines, or need to defend, explain, interpret, or influence another to see anything differently? The Sabbath glories in the goodness, the amazing, solicitous, heart-thrilling glory of each person to whom we are privileged to speak on that day.

Imagine seeing your spouse (or child, parent, friend, neighbor) and for one day, for twenty-four hours, not denying the tensions or heartache or unrequited desire, yet looking beyond those struggles to the promise of an utterly glorious and utterly redeemed spouse and perfected marriage. And then, miracle beyond comprehension and privilege, what would it be like to spend a full day with a person imbued with such glory? What would happen to a friendship, if for one day, just twenty-four hours, we put aside our struggles and celebrated what brought us together and what has enabled us to remain as friends? Even more, what would happen if we were to see the other, *now*, in the light of the glory they will one day be? As C. S. Lewis states, "You have never talked to a mere mortal."[2]

The Sabbath is the day we set aside to look at one another from the vantage point of eternity and then to operate in time, in an actual hour or minute, as if it is true. What might it look like if we lived as if we will not be endlessly divided from those who have brought us harm and whom we have failed as well?

PRACTICING ETERNITY

The Sabbath is like walking on the high wire or swinging on the trapeze with the assuring safety net strung below. We get to swing and try our hand at catapulting our body from the bar to the waiting hands of the other, knowing the worst that can happen is an exhilarating fall to a well-apportioned safety net. Why would we not go play? To practice eternity on the Sabbath, we must give way to curiosity, coziness, and care.

CURIOSITY

Accusations bring suspicion and paranoia. The effect of all division brings a kind of hypervigilance that arrests the joy of surprise and wonder. It is impossible to receive the day when one is exhausted with the debris of judging oneself and others. How can I celebrate a Sabbath, let alone the queen of joy, when my heart is riddled with the weariness of suspicion?

Curiosity is a gift of the Spirit. It loves to be taken as a guest into the chambers of wonder to be humbled and lifted up only to ask, *Is there more?* The question of what is more is asked either out of greed or wonder. If asked out of greed, then nothing will satisfy and there will be no rest—only linear, focused, unrelenting ambition. If what motivates the heart is the delight in wonder, then the desire for more will prompt a complex search that ends up with fascinating connections, interplay, and unity.

Ambition leads to the demand for the shortest path between points to gain the most in the least amount of time; wonder calls the heart to explore the unexpected, nonlinear paths that often create a new unity that could not be expected when one first began. One Sabbath my wife asked me, "If we were to pray today for our enemies, who do you most hope to be united with on this earth? And who do you most hope not to see until heaven?" I nearly choked. Her questions were brilliant. She was asking, "Who do you most miss and who has hurt you the most?" Instead of pretending I have no enemies, she was inviting me to explore, to be curious about my enemies and to enter into a conversation that took me far beyond the typical guilt ("I should do something") or hopelessness ("I can't do anything"). I began to play with the question—what does it mean to care again for my enemies? I will one day be face to face with each of my enemies—why not begin today to imagine what it will be like with them?

Norman Wirzba brilliantly states, "The Sabbath asks us to notice."[3] Our eyes are meant to be wide open on this day, looking for the shadow of the glorious substance ahead. If we are curiously open to delight, our senses will draw us to the infinite domain of beauty, goodness, and truth.

COZINESS

The tenser the situation, the less likely we will kick back and be ourselves. The Sabbath is the day not merely to relax or rest, but to get cozy. It is our day to not only be curious about enemies, astronomy, plant mitosis, black holes, or which trail may be the best to go bow hunting on later in the fall, but to do so in our pajamas or lying in a hammock or walking with our dearest friend. It is a day of rich and abiding safety. The question to be asked is, "What would give you the greatest sense of the abiding goodness of the Father's arms?"

I recall one Sabbath when I was stricken with a severe cold. I wanted to be surrounded by the covers and release the need to get going—for some reason I couldn't. Becky came in and said, "You are staying in bed. When I return, I will have a surprise for you." I borrowed her strength on my behalf and fell back to sleep. A bit later, she showed up with an armful of magazines.

They spanned the gambit from sailing, fly-fishing, motorcycling, and *Colonial Homes*. I devoured the pointless print like it was chicken soup and waxed in and out of sleep for the day. Our lives are so seldom spent with cozy clothes, people, and places.

A Sabbath is a safe and cozy day to explore. This doesn't imply that a Sabbath has no risk or danger—it is danger chosen as fitting our comfort. The conversation about my enemies was not easy; in fact, it was full of the unknown. Yet my wife set the conversation in a frame that intrigued me and allowed me to talk and pray without pressure or guilt.

CARE

The Sabbath is also a day to receive and offer care. If peace is the promise of Sabbath, then there is no need to make progress on long-term conflicts or attempt to resolve current struggles. We do not allow it to be a day to make decisions or plan for the exigencies of work. The Sabbath is a day to care for one another and all those we are privileged to celebrate.

Madeleine Bunting names our problem with human sustainability. She says, "Human sustainability lies in the question 'Who found time to care for whom?'"[4] Who will care for you as you age? A dear friend sat for months in a nursing home caring for her dying mother because of the paucity of care. Her mother was in the finest facility in their city at a cost of well over a hundred thousand dollars a year. Yet when the daughter was absent for even one day, she observed clear signs of neglect. Care can seldom, if ever, be purchased, because it requires a commitment of honor.

To care means to tend to something with diligence and delight. To care for a plant is to provide it with good soil, food, and sunlight. Can it be that different with one's son or daughter, husband or wife, and friends? To care means I have checked in with my plant to notice the brown edges on the leaves or the soggy soil. I tend—time, focus, concern—for what I care. I also delight in the new growth and can measure the progress from one frame to the other. I study what I love—and if I love what I study, then a union occurs between the object and the subject. Sabbath is a joyful union, at one, connected and in, at, and with peace.

Sabbath is a joyful union, at one,
connected and in, at, and with peace.

7

SABBATH PLAY: DESTITUTION SURRENDERS TO ABUNDANCE

IT IS HARD TO KNOW WHICH IS WORSE—TO BE ALONE OR to be bereft. There are communities of poverty that somehow sustain themselves, albeit with little. There are societies of plenty that are based on disposability and shifting alliances of profitability. One only need recall the statement "In Washington, DC, if you want a friend, buy a dog" to comprehend the loneliness that is related to the whims of the electorate and the vagaries of power. Nothing can be as unimaginable as being hungry and empty while simultaneously being an outcast even to the poor and marginalized. Perhaps only a leper understands what it means to be both destitute and despised.

We desperately need both to be connected to others and to

have a full belly. Sadly, those in the West seldom consider the fundamental importance of a full belly or the cost of living with the uncertainty of whether we can provide for ourselves and our families. Destitution is not a big issue for those able to buy and read this book—not really. Seldom do the average buyers of religious literature venture into a soup kitchen, let alone suffer true poverty and uncertainty about whether there will be food today. So what does it mean to enter the Sabbath as a refuge from destitution?

We desperately need both to be connected to others and to have a full belly.

MIDDLE-CLASS DESTITUTION

There are two categories of destitution that are real for the middle class: 1) the emptiness of an uncertain future and 2) the emptiness of the unrealized present. These issues are not the sole domain of the middle class, yet they are often uniquely felt by those who are neither poor nor rich.

There are many in the middle (and upper) class who live in plenty on the basis of plastic. It is not uncommon in our day for a two-income family to be only a few paychecks from bankruptcy. There are many families who live in lovely houses and yet pay for their groceries with credit cards because their cash flow is so low. We are a nation that lives beyond its means, doesn't provide for its future, and banks on its past to live excessively in the present.

If both breadwinners lost their jobs, how long would their savings last before they became destitute? Most of us don't consider this a real possibility. Perhaps the looming recession will pass us by unscathed, or it may hit us as profoundly as being run down crossing on a green light. And that is another issue: the unknown illnesses and accidents that destroy, steal, and kill a life in an instant. Who knows whether tomorrow you will be able to work when you get the diagnosis of cancer or a car accident that keeps you from being able to provide for your family? We all live with and in constant, chronic uncertainty.

If finances prompt uncertainty, then how much more so do relationships gnaw on us? Will our child return to God? Will we ever see passion return to our marriage? How are we to live with the emptiness that can't even be named in many of our churches without fear of greater judgment and alienation? Our relational future haunts us.

We also live with the gnawing awareness of our unrealized present. There are few people living their dream—fewer people who allow themselves to dream something other than the conventional American dream. We all wanted to be dancers, rock stars, professional athletes, millionaires, or at least happily married with 2.2 children. The majority of people acknowledge that life is a far cry from what they thought it would be twenty or thirty years ago. Yet there are people who succeed as dancers, rock stars, and pro athletes; there are people who seem to have happy families. And we envy them, strive after our version of success, and become slaves to systems that debase us.

ENVY

Envy is the craving to possess what another owns in order to fill our desperate emptiness. We want their book contract, prestige, thin thighs, beautiful hair, new Mercedes. And it is usually not enough to have something similar or slightly less than what they own—it has to be bigger and better. A wise man once observed, "Most people are motivated to success because they envy their neighbors. But this, too, is meaningless—like chasing the wind" (Eccl. 4:4). It can be said market-driven economies depend on this desire for their impetus to sell the next best thing. When one looks deeper into the dark hole of envy, it is far crueler than merely the desire to better oneself.

The deepest envy desires to take from the other what they possess in order to bask before their humiliation. We have determined that our destitution will only be resolved if we can simultaneously deprive our rivals of their goods and possess what they own.

Envy gnaws at the core and makes us sick. We often use the color green to describe the intense craving to possess what another owns. "I am green with envy." The color is not an indication of growth or life; instead, it clearly implies swirling nausea and destabilizing sickness. We can become delirious with envy to the degree people have killed others or plotted their destruction through campaigns of slander. It blinds the heart to anything but the joy of depriving the other of joy.

STRIVING

We chase after wind, fools we are. "'Better to have one handful with quietness than two handfuls with hard work and chasing the wind'" (Eccl. 4:6). We strive to catch the wind and it blows through our hands time again, yet do we learn? We pocket one more responsibility and say to ourselves, "This busy season will certainly slow down in time." Yet I have met men who in their seventies confess they thought by that age life would have taken on a different hue, but it hasn't because they continue to press on toward a goal that has little to do with the Sabbath.

Striving is always a noisy activity. It generates heat, din, and bluster. One can almost always tell important people by their chronic commitment to keeping time and moving the agenda ahead. The more important one perceives oneself, the more necessary it is to keep advancing toward the destination. There is no time for meandering. There is no place for saying, "Enough, truly. I have enough money, enough books, enough travel. I have enough. It is time to give away all that I am, all that I have." Whenever one is in need of more and operates with the noise of striving, there will be a senseless surrender to addiction.

SLAVERY

Whomever we envy will become an enemy; what they possess becomes an addiction. Slowly and surely, we get mired by our obsession to obtain, to gain, to control. It becomes a goal: "I need a new hot tub like my neighbor." We purchase one that makes the neighbor's look like a hole in the ground. There is satisfaction—yes, yet only for a brief season. But it is lost as soon as we see what others are enjoying that surpasses our status. Without notice, we become consumers not of products or even experiences, but of status. We are addicted to seeing ourselves as at least equal to if not beyond our peers. We become whores to gods that are not God.

Most people who have affairs say it was not for the sex or because life at home was lacking—they simply wanted companionship without commitment and a touch of sassy wildness to spice up their humdrum life. It is the slogan of an entire city and industry: "What happens in Las Vegas, stays in Las Vegas." We sell excess experience as a means of filling hollowness. And it doesn't work. The only means to escape the hollow futility of another fun night is to suborn desire to duty and dreams to reality. And it doesn't work. The flight to fancy and the hard landing of necessity are two sides of the same coin that are the binary of a life without Sabbath. Sabbath frees us from this duality through playful obedience to abundance.

CREATIONAL ABUNDANCE

The earth is bubbling with the presence of God. It teems, swims, gurgles, and cries out, "Holy, holy, holy!"—without speaking a word. And its abundance is so ripe and full that it is impossible to ignore. As the psalmist said,

> The heavens proclaim the glory of God
>> The skies display his craftsmanship.
> Day after day they continue to speak;
>> night after night they make him known. (Ps. 19:1–2)

I flew from snowy Appleton, Wisconsin, to sunny Atlanta in early March. The warmth and early green buds and the fragrant wafts of spring seized me while I stood outside, face to the sun, for ten minutes waiting for my coach to pick me up. It was only hours before that I stood next to six-foot snow banks and shivered waiting for another driver to pick me up. We are surrounded by God's delight in extremity and abundance.

Wake up and smell the air. Feel the loam loosen in your hands as you rub dirt between your fingers. Taste the explosion of sensation as you bite into an orange slice. The creation is an orchestral oratory arranged as an invitation to bring our voice to the song as praise. And the abundance of creation pales in comparison to the superabundance of re-creation.

The earth is bubbling with the presence of God . . .
and its abundance is so ripe and full that it is impossible to ignore.

RE-CREATION'S SUPERABUNDANCE

The abundance of creation is given steroids in the new heavens and earth. Listen to how two Old Testament prophets describe it:

"This river flows east through the desert into the valley of the Dead Sea. The waters of this stream will make the salty waters of the Dead Sea fresh and pure. There will be swarms of living things wherever the water of this river flows. Fish will abound in the Dead Sea, for its waters will become fresh. Life will flourish wherever this water flows." (Ezek. 47:8–9)

In that day the mountains will drip with sweet wine,
    and the hills will flow with milk.
Water will fill the streambeds of Judah,
        and a fountain will burst forth from the LORD's Temple,
        watering the arid valley of acacias. (Joel 3:18)

It isn't just water that spills down the ravines and gushes down the mountains; instead, wine and milk fill the streambeds. Wine will drip down the mountains in a torrent of robust joy. And the water will be so pure and bountiful that it will fill the Dead Sea with fresh water, and fish will live in what once was inhabitable. Life will flourish because there will be a continual stream that explodes from the temple watering all the arid valleys and hearts on the earth.

This is all hyperbole—how else does one communicate the inexpressible? Belden Lane tells the story of the French bringing a handful of desert Bedouin leaders to Paris to see the glory of their culture. They saw the Eiffel Tower and other architectural delights with polite boredom. But when taken to see a waterfall in the countryside, they stood in utter amazement. They waited for the surging flow to stop. "They refused to leave, adamantly declaring to their French guide that honor required waiting . . . waiting for the end. Knowing the water could not last much longer, they awaited the moment 'when God would grow weary of his madness,' when this wild extravagance would suddenly and finally exhaust itself."[1]

Nothing they had seen in their world paralleled a gushing flow of water that had run endlessly for thousands of years. We are the Bedouins who have learned to live in the desert of God's absence for thousands of years, who cannot imagine the inexhaustible glory that has already been given to us in Jesus, that pours through the cross and will pour forth with utter glory when he gloriously returns. The Sabbath gives us the opportunity to stand before the endless outpouring of superabundance and fill up our thimble of faith with a drop of the bounty ahead.

LIFTING A THIMBLE

I heard pastor John MacArthur say that preaching was like taking a bucket of water and pouring it into the thimbles of those who hear, only for them to spill their water on the way out of church. I have felt that way with some of my best lectures, but I suspect, at least with a few, I am wrong. In fact, I bet some actually clink their thimbles with their mates and sing a good Kiwi drinking song. The Sabbath is a party, and what is a good party without a drinking song? Almost all the early John Wesley hymns were sung to what at the time was wild pub music.

I am currently writing much of this chapter to the music of Eddie Vedder, and in my hearing he celebrates the feminine wisdom of God, the receiving heart of love that is greater than the big hard sun beating down in the big, hard world.[2] I'm listening to this music to mock death.

I just received word that a young and glorious woman, a practicum facilitator at Mars Hill Graduate School, died of a brain aneurism. I heard this news while I was writing in the Red Carpet Club in Atlanta, and I burst into tears. Executives and businessmen and women stared at me like a pariah who soiled the sanctity of their silence.

I needed to retreat. I needed to surround myself with something that brought comfort and solace, and I knew the song I needed to hear. I needed to raise a glass to a comrade who had passed from this earth, a colleague whom I both respect and envy. She is home; I am not. She is glorified; I am far, far from it. I can only cry; she is laughing, dancing, wildly free, and beaming with the roaring wet glory that has enveloped her being. I need music. She is music. She sings to Jesus, and he is dancing with her in his arms. The party has begun.

Sabbath raises a small thimble to glory and says, "Thank you, thank you." Gratitude is our only response to what pours out on our behalf. When we have tasted his love for us amid the heartache of this world, then we can let him sing to us as we sing him as the only song that can fill us.

Sabbath raises a small thimble to glory
and says, "Thank you, thank you."

OFFERING BREAD AND WINE

Abundance is not about possession; it is utterly, completely, and solely about gratitude. The richest men or women on this earth are paupers if they are not recklessly stunned by the gift of their good fortune. It is not really theirs—it is God's treasure, given to us. It is not due to their brilliance or hard work; it is due to the gift of God. It is not the result of fortune or luck; it is the sovereign will of God—that is, his sweet pleasure. The poorest man or woman on this earth is richer than the wealthiest if there is gratitude for the plate of rice and beans.

What is most humbling, almost beyond words, is to be with the poor, who gratefully give to those who in comparison seem to own the stars and the moon. The data about donations in the United States is staggering. Those who make more than $100,000 a year give less than 1.3 percent. Those who make $35,000 to $50,000 often give as high as 7 percent.[3]

What are we to learn from this data? The Sabbath is not a vacation; it is a grateful celebration. Who are you celebrating? To whom do you owe your life, your current taste of re-creation? Who marked you with kindness that has enabled you to offer care in return? Who has scarred you with heartache that has enabled you to enter the wounds of others with grace? We are called to bless those who love us and those who love to do us harm. Both groups escort us to the banquet of God, served on the Cross, for those who are not ashamed to be beggars and even less ashamed to be called sons and daughters of God.

SABBATH BREAD

The Sabbath is the moment to measure the meaning of his body offered to me. If I am grateful for the flurry of birds that race by my window, how much more am I stunned silly by the burst of God through a son born to a virgin? How do I take in the bread of his flesh offered to me to taste the salt and dough of his laughter, tears, anger, and kindness? I don't know how to ponder the incarnation beyond pondering the utter fullness, the superabundance of his humanity. Jesus is the fullness of what it means to be peculiarly human. He is abrupt, kind, generous, angry, full of sorrow, tempted, faithful, and alive, so alive it makes my head spin.

The more I ponder the person of Jesus and ask him to speak to my heart—directly with words from his mouth for me, just me—the more I hear words that can be communicated yet never bear the same sweetness in their sharing that I taste in their reception. The more I ask Jesus to speak to my heart—indirectly through Chagall, Sufjan Stevens, and the conversation I'm listening to as I write in an airport—the more I am stunned by not only how the heavens declare his glory, but how so do all who inhabit the earth.

> *The more I ask Jesus to speak to my heart . . . the more I am stunned by not only how the heavens declare his glory, but how so do all who inhabit the earth.*

I not only get to taste the rare bread of his presence on the Sabbath, but I also get to offer to those with whom I celebrate the abundance of the Creator. In our family, Sabbath has been our day to write or call those whom we most owe gratitude—

friends, enemies, strangers, acquaintances, the dead and the living. The letters never need to be sent—some are winged away on Monday, yet to offer in black and white the bread of praise, we are reconnected to those who have marked us with God.

The Sabbath is also the day my wife and I read to each other from texts that have touched us during the week. These passages are the incarnate bread we feed each other. How do I know what is sparking life in my wife unless we create space to light up the world? Our reading to each other is a gift of little nothings. What nothings—meaning non-thing gifts including gifts of care, time, reflection, education, and experience—do you offer to those with whom you celebrate Sabbath?

For countless reasons, I never learned to cook. I am old, but I am not utterly incompetent. I asked my wife to help me learn to cook several fine meals. We studied the texts of cookbooks and settled on several meals that I can now prepare with some degree of joy. Part of our Sabbath on Saturday night is often spent preparing a meal together (she is the overseer). The meal suffices with leftovers for Sunday lunch and dinner (with a few variations). The bread of gratitude is meant to be offered to each other and taken as his body broken on our behalf. But we were meant not only to eat, but to drink gratitude.

SABBATH WINE

Wine sweetens life; it "gladdens the heart" (Ps. 104:15 NIV). *Gladdening* is a word for intoxicated self-forgetfulness. There are many words for intoxication in the Bible, and the phrase "glad-dening the heart" implies a sweet, slight rounding of the edges, a warm, gentle buzz. A friend has started a brewery—Two Beers Brewing Co.—with the motto: "All conversations go bet-ter with two beers."[4] It takes the edge off, doesn't distort with true intoxication, and allows an entry into pleasure that may not be possible without the dollop of a small draft.

As I mentioned earlier, a year ago I was diagnosed with prediabetes. It requires I give up alcohol, sugar, and starch. I've lost fifty pounds and much pleasure. But in the process I have found that wine, too, is a metaphor. I can't drink fine or dirt-cheap wine (at least not often), yet there are many ways to enter into the sweet gratitude of Sabbath wine.

A friend savors the writings of Wallace Stegner. She doesn't read him during the week and saves her entry to his words for the Sabbath. Another friend plays on her recorder music that is savory to her heart. Often on a Sabbath, I string up my four-weight Orvis rod and go out to our backyard and step into the waters of forgetfulness and memory. I know the river—I won't tell you; it is a gift, a secret. I step just a hundred yards ahead of the hole that Stan named after me. I prepare to drop my fly just to the right of the boulder that is ten feet off the bank. There is a monster trout lurking in the shadows. We saw it when Don hooked a sixteen-inch cutthroat, and after a brief fight, it was devoured by the monster bull trout that owns that domain.

The movement of the wand in my hand is a rhythm of

beauty that soothes; the sensuous silk of solace is as close as my embodied imagination. The Lord of the Sabbath says, "'The Sabbath was made for man, not man for the Sabbath'" (Mark 2:27 NIV). Take and eat; take and drink—all to glory.

8

SABBATH PLAY: DESPAIR SURRENDERS TO JOY

SABBATH CALLS US TO ACT AGAINST DIVISION AND DESTI-
tution—defying it through the celebration of peace and abundance. We are invited to write the script for our character each
week, to act on the stage of Sabbath a new play of redemption.
We are to pretend, to play as if the new heavens and earth have
dawned and all despair and death have been swallowed into the
glory of the resurrection. For Christians the Sabbath is the day
we play in the light of untrammeled freshness.

It is the day that despair and death surrender to joy. We
need to consider how despair quietly seeps into our day like
carbon dioxide, unnoticed, until one falls into a death sleep.
Then we will ponder how this day of peace and abundance is
meant to be a celebration of joy.

DESPAIR: A HATRED OF HOPE

Hope extends us beyond our current moment of suffering to imagine a time in which our deepest desire is not only satisfied but taken beyond our wildest dreams. There are lesser dreams that we can attain that usually involve an increase in pleasure. For example, I want to own a sailboat. The kind I'd like to buy is infinitely beyond my means, but I have my eye on a nineteen-foot sailboat that I could take out on a whim. I have already saved a third of the cost, and within several years I should have enough to make the purchase. This is a purchasable dream based on "work." Any dream we can obtain by hard work has value, but it is not the kind of hope we tend to hate. We hate hope that calls us to labor rather than merely to work.

Lewis Hyde compares work and labor. He wrote, "Work is what we do by the hour. . . . Labor, on the other hand, sets its own pace. Work is an intended activity that is accomplished through the will. A labor can be intended but only to the extent of doing the groundwork, or of not doing things that would clearly prevent the labor. And labor, because it sets its own pace, is usually accompanied by idleness, leisure, even sleep."[1]

How do we articulate the difference between labor that gives life and work that extinguishes hope? It may be as simple as saying all labor is done to create something that goes beyond the completion of a task—it seeks a connectedness to someone for something greater than mere compensation.

Work is painting a wall; labor is starting a painting business so that one can choose how a job will be finished with integrity. Work is taking a literature class; labor is writing a poem to address the death of one's parent. Working allows us to control the outcome and therefore achieve our manageable dreams. Labor calls us to risk our dreams without much control to create something that goes beyond what we can imagine. It is labor, not work, that we hate. We prefer to kill the hope of what labor may bring forth rather than to risk so much for possibly so little.

> *Labor calls us to risk our dreams without much control to create something that goes beyond what we can imagine.*

I was asked by a spiritual director to sit in the same seat for a full morning, outdoors, and wait to see what God had to say. Was I willing to spend a day sitting and waiting, listening and remaining open? What if nothing happened and I felt foolish that I had hoped and been left empty? We are willing to work our lives away, yet we are terrified to labor; the Sabbath prepares us to labor and to eschew work.

Our deepest hope is for reconciliation and restoration; for fullness and completeness of being. And these dreams are not purchasable, though if they are to be achieved, it must come from hope's labor. But what keeps us from desiring and laboring in hope and instead working to kill hope? In part, the answer is regret related to division and worry associated with destitution. Despair, in large measure, is the killing of hope because there is no rest from accusation and emptiness.

REGRET: THE DARK FRUIT OF ACCUSATION

Division brings accusation and with it regret. *Why did I say the sentence that ruptured our friendship? Why did we move to Seattle? Why didn't I make the call that might have salvaged my job?* Accusation leads to the burdensome ruminations that we call regret.

Regret returns us to the burned-down remains of the past with sorrow that has no end or point. We walk through the charred house and remember how good it once was and how we failed. Regret will often prompt a replay of all that happened with the illusion that only one small thing needed to happen to have kept the tragedy from occurring. And then our thoughts wander to *Why?* and *If only . . .*

Regret makes no attempt to learn from the past, or even to replay it with an eye to understand what processes were involved, in order to address those same recurrent issues. Instead, regret wallows in despair, assuming fate has pointed its fickle finger in my face and that I am bound to this moment and nothing can be done to change it. Regret drinks despair as a solace against true hope. But its drinking buddy, worry, is almost always nearby to offer peanuts to increase the thirst for more despair.

WORRY: THE DARK FRUIT OF EMPTINESS

What will become of me if I don't . . . get married, have a child, get the promotion, lose weight, overcome my addiction, or deal with my marriage? The list is endless. I know people who worry they will not be able to stop worrying. I know people who can't fall asleep because they are worrying about not being able to sleep. It is a vicious cycle; the catch-22 of worry is malevolent. Worry takes on a life of its own and parasitically devours us as it thrives.

Worry is the fear of emptiness. We think, *How will I live if I am called to suffer in this way without end and with no clarity or explanation?* Worry makes no attempt to move into the unknown with conviction and courage. Instead, it obsesses about how our life will be ruined if certain factors outside of our control do not change. Worry extends regret to the future as it anticipates a sorrow too great to endure.

For this reason, worry is anti-Sabbath. Sabbath requires the release of worry and invites us to trust. Both regret and worry assume there is no God, or at least not one who loves and pours himself out for his children. Both worry and regret are satanic.

Worry is anti-Sabbath.

Despair refuses to grieve the mistakes of the past and be grateful for the finished work of Christ that opens a new vista for my future. Despair refuses to anticipate and dream the new future for fear that it will simply go awry again. Hope opens us to the future and seizes opportunity to redeem dreams.

DESPAIR'S CHILDREN

Despair can appear in many different forms. The most obvious is its biological sibling, depression. Depression almost always involves some degree of regret and worry, yet it is first and foremost a biological issue that needs to be treated with antidepressant medication. In addition, those who are depressed must enter the terrain of their hatred of hope. But there are many who live in despair, that don't suffer depression or even appear to be unhappy. In our day, despair shows itself in cynicism, conventionality, and consumerism.

CYNICISM

It is hip to be cynical. It is the *lingua franca* of the day. There is a disdain for innocence, even for childhood. I once heard a mother-to-be tell her husband that their daughter could be a child until age five or six, and then she would need to get ready for the demands of life. She would go to one of the best kindergartens and elementary schools. Her young future was already laid out with nannies, lessons, summer excursions, and learning opportunities.

Cynicism breeds contempt and greater alienation, or

division. It leads to a greater need to control life so the innocent wonder of gratitude never opens the heart to want to serve. Cynicism never needs to labor for goodness; it is too busy deconstructing all pretenders.

CONVENTIONALITY

Conventional behavior is living life as a prepackaged, paint-in-the-numbers craft kit. It requires no creativity or hope, only dutiful obedience to whatever "truth" or "leader" or "truth leader" that enables one to escape the onus of freedom. This can occur among liberals, conservatives, Democrats, Republicans, anarchists, skinheads, gay-rights activists, and gay opponents. It involves any form of dogmatism where the party line is uncritically accepted as the superior truth to all other claimants.

Often the "truth" provides a set of parameters that shape nearly every dimension of life, including dress code, acceptable art, and use of time and money. The benefit is that the adherents get to live vicariously through the lives of their heroes rather than getting dirty in a game that requires deep-rooted hope to play. In many ways, those who are happy to be blind live the deepest form of hopelessness, because they have not even identified their fear of hope.

CONSUMERISM

In addition to the other kinds of cultural despair, another is the discontent endemic to consumerism. I have an excellent cell phone that enables me to get e-mail, connect to the Internet, take photos and videos, and occasionally make and receive phone calls. But my heart is allured to another phone. I don't need it; I want it. Why do I want it? Because it is cool. One can make pictures on the screen pass quickly with the touch of a finger. My old phone is viable, yet the new phone holds the promise of a new day without limit or flaw.

Consumerism hope is about realized desire that can be worked for without any need to labor. If the materialistic desires are sufficiently extensive and expensive, then hope for the attainable can be put off long enough to counterfeit the long-term perseverance required for any labored hope. Despair rises as repeated purchases end with boredom rather than gratitude.

GRATITUDE AND DESPAIR

Cynicism, conventionalism, and consumerism—and all other forms of despair—are at war with gratitude. The more I receive every dimension of life as a gift, the less likely I am to feel entitled and irritated when I don't get what I want. I believe there is a profound correlation between gratitude and joy and the absence of gratitude and despair.

Despair is like an endless drive on a cul-de-sac. One sees the same terrain again and again with no hope or anticipation of anything new. We desire novelty and new experience, yet we are deadened to looking outside our tight circle for what our heart most deeply desires. Despair robs the heart of imagination. The book of Ecclesiastes tells us, indeed, there is nothing new under the sun, except redemption. The sun breaking in on a cloudy winter Seattle day can be received as a nice break from the gloom or as something more. It can be engaged as a breaking in of a goodness that gives a taste of God's invisible qualities (Rom. 1:20). We see the character of God whenever we are grateful.

Gratitude opens the heart not only to wonder but to freedom. Anything that stirs gratitude opens our eyes to a world outside our seeing. It is similar to the first time I looked into a top-quality home telescope and could see galaxies I had never noticed. My friend guided my eyes to see solar systems that were infinitely beyond what the naked eye could see. I was in awe and couldn't wait to reenter the new world every time we were in his home.

Gratitude opens the heart not only to wonder but to freedom.

When a gift is received, it conceives a debt in us that must grow full-term before the debt can be birthed and the gift given away to another. Whatever the gift, it is greater than the one who receives it, and we must grow to become equal to the gift we have received. Lewis Hyde says, "A gift that has the power to change us awakens a part of the soul. But we cannot receive the gift until we can meet it as an equal. We therefore submit ourselves to the labor becoming like the gift. Giving a return gift is the final act in the labor of gratitude, and it is also, there-fore, the true acceptance of the original gift."[2]

There is a burden of gratitude that, if it is not returned, will crush our spirits or splinter them. But we don't give to get rid of the burden; we must become like the gift in order to give it in its fullness. Consider the insistence of the young convert (to anything). The inexperienced convert wants everyone to know or try what he has found as life-changing. Usually the gift of the convert's passion is neither ripe nor ready to be eaten. The effect is usually irritating rather than motivating. Gratitude must grow full-term before the gift can produce joy.

SABBATH JOY

Joy is a conundrum that often, like delight, is too terrifying to embrace. We claim we want joy, yet few are willing to earn the right to receive it as a gift. Sabbath joy is not gained by showing up with new shoes, running shorts, and the sincere intention to run a marathon. No one would expect to run a marathon on the first day of training, no matter how strong the desire. Joy is cho-sen, and one prepares for its arrival by rigorous suffering.

Do you want joy? Then open your heart to suffer. Suffering involves the ruthless paring away of all that will keep joy at bay. We seem to prefer regret and worry to joy. We'd prefer to slouch away the day and not enter into a dialogue about the delight of peace and abundance—it is easier to wish and whine, to long for something and then to lament its absence. The power of whining is that we simultaneously feel laden with desire and then make someone (including ourselves) pay for our wretched luck.

Joy must be chosen, but the deeper conundrum is that it can't be controlled or cajoled as to when it will come or how long it will stay.[3] What is joy? I can no more define joy than I can beauty. Perhaps it is best to say that joy is a touch of sweet madness that comes when we sense God is closer to us than our own heartbeats.

Sabbath joy is far deeper than mere pleasure, or even happiness, or lightness of being. Joy has little to do with moments of success, reward, or honor. It is related to circumstances, yet it is not centered on something working out well. In fact, most of my joy has come within the frame of dark and troubling times. It has come in the midst of heartache and confusion. It seems uniquely related to death—death of a friend or even a friendship, the death of dream or an illusion that masqueraded as a worthy desire. Death has been the inevitable frame for joy.

Sabbath is not an escape from death. Instead, Sabbath is the promise that death doesn't win. Sabbath is not a turning from death and pretending it doesn't mar us; instead, we are to act before death as if has no ultimate power.

My wife and I were taking a Sabbath walk and talking about a disappointing time she had with a friend. The more we talked, the more I could feel death creeping in to take us away from the day. It was an important conversation, and I didn't want to say, "This is not a Sabbath conversation"—but I knew our pleasure in being together was waning. I asked her, "If we both believed there was joy in knowing Christ and the power of his resurrection and the fellowship of sharing in his suffering— what do you think would be different about this conversation?"

Neither of us had a clue. She at first felt defensive. I felt stuck. We could escape to a more pleasant conversation, yet that would give death another victory. Sabbath joy requires the exercise of starts and stops, failing and then getting back up to mock despair. Becky suggested we walk and quietly pray and listen to the pulse of goodness in the forest surrounding us. After a while, she said, "My friend is full of accusations and hurt. And I didn't want to stop her assault for fear that her fury would get worse. I endured her, and I didn't really care for her."

I listened to her words and watched her face. She was telling the truth, yet there was no sign of wonder or joy. She had made the shift from being irritated by her friend to accepting her failure. All I knew to do was to ask, "Are we any closer to joy?" She smiled and said, "Leave me alone, Mr. Sabbath." We started laughing. Her smile returned and the twinkle in her eye was enough for me to see the clouds had lifted and the sun was again shining. Such an utterly insignificant moment passed, and we reentered the conversation with far more curiosity and care.

Our joy in Sabbath is almost entirely bound to those with whom we spend the day. I simply wouldn't want to spend the day with anyone who does not consciously and intentionally mock death by not giving into the gravitational pull of despair. Choose carefully your company on this one, most holy day. There is no one on this earth with whom I have more joy than being with my bride of more than thirty years. She reflects the Sabbath courage to weep in the other six days and to laugh at death's claim to be the final word.

But the Sabbath is meant as a feast for a far wider circle of companions than just a few. What is imperative is not the number, but the quality of those who sit at the table. Dine with those who are unafraid of sorrow and joy or their presence together.

> *The Sabbath is meant as a feast for a far wider circle of companions than just a few.*

The apostle Paul said our joy comes as we pour ourselves out like the crucified One. He writes, "But I will rejoice even if I lose my life, pouring it out like a liquid offering to God, just like your faithful service is an offering to God. And I want all of you to share that joy. Yes, you should rejoice, and I will share your joy" (Phil. 2:17–18).

What is our Sabbath joy? We are gifted to enter God's delight in spite of the debris of death. Our joy is in celebrating that love is stronger than death; and the madness of God is saner than the wisdom of man. Joy is in being a drink offering, poured out to give life. Death not only doesn't win; death becomes the only framework for freedom. Our heartache is a drama that tells not only our story, but also the story of the death and resurrection.

Our joy is simple. We occasionally get a glimpse of the greater story our lives get to tell and hear the director, God, bless us with his delight. The joy of this remarkable day is to clear away the space of the rest of the week to turn our senses to God's delight, not merely in creation but for us. God intends to speak a matchless, free, fresh blessing to each of his creatures and pour out on our behalf his joy, "Look and see, my beloved son, my beloved daughter."

We are to clear away on this day all the debris from the past week and the week ahead—and turn our ears to his delight. We are to labor, not work, to stretch ourselves out on a couch with a soft pillow and quiet our heart to ask, "What do you wish to say to me, King of kings, Abba Father, Daddy?" It is not presumptuous to ask, "What is it that you see in me that brings you delight?"

The bold risk of hope is to anticipate with joy the words God longs for us to hear with peace and abundance. Sabbath joy turns the words of accusation to praise and the emptiness of destitution to a celebration of his overflowing kindness for his Sabbath sons and daughters.

PART 3

SABBATH PERFORMANCE

9

ACTING OUT
SABBATH IN RITUAL
AND SYMBOL

WE SETTLED IN OUR SEATS FOR THE PLAY TO BEGIN. Sadly, we had purchased tickets far too late, and the six of us sat in seats spread throughout the large theater. Prior to arrival we picked the tickets out of a hat. Our son, Andrew, got a seat that appeared to be in the far back of the balcony. He was nonchalant; he had not wanted to waste his time going to a play, and so to be a million miles away from the action fit his nineteen-year-old soul.

My seat was about eight rows from the front, well to the right. I knew it was pointless to look for Andrew, but after I had been seated for five minutes I saw him saunter to the front row. He looked smug and happy. I saw him sit in the middle of the front row, mere feet from the stage.

At intermission I grabbed him and demanded he give me

his seat since he didn't care where he sat. He looked at me like a mosquito and whapped me on the arm. No deal. His face glowed with delight. He gloried in the sweat and saliva of the actors like he was at a pro wrestling event. It gripped him. It is meant to—theater is our life.

THE WORLD IS A STAGE

Shakespeare grasped the profound intrigue the theater holds for humanity. Originally the theater was a lower-class, commoner experience that the educated and religious saw as base and degrading. Theater was not written for the intelligentsia or the erudite—it was meant to grip the plowman, carpenter, and maidservant.

The theater holds intrigue because it allows us to see our stories—the dilemma of our existence—without crossing the threshold into reality. Yet it is so close that we can see real characters, with endless dialogue, just like ours, suffer and triumph in a brief period of time. Unlike a movie that may at one level seem more real because the stage is less "staged." Nonetheless, the celluloid two-dimensionality of the medium allows us to be even more distant from the drama.

A play places us on the stage as an actor in our life, and the grip of a good play doesn't end even after it is finished. We intuitively sense that the drama on stage intersects our life; it bleeds into the role we feel bound to play. There are few who have considered the intersection of theology and theater more profoundly than Hans Urs Von Balthasar. He wrote, "God does not want to be just 'contemplated' and 'perceived' by us, like a solitary actor by his public; no, from the beginning he has provided for a play in which we all must share."[1]

GOD IS AN ACTOR

God intends for us to see our lives in the light of an eternal drama. We each not only have a character and a role in an evolving script, but a life to be lived for the larger story that is meant to reveal something about the nature of the human condition. What is incomprehensible is not that we are in God's play, but that he is in ours. Balthasar wrote, "The play belongs to God and he participates in it, or he invites us to participate in his play. He made the stage which is the world and yet the world has developed its own play with its own actors and stories. Nonetheless, he wishes to play on our stage. It is a case of the play within the play: our play 'plays' in his play."[2]

We are in God's play, yet our rebellion creates a drama that requires God to enter our play in an act that goes far beyond linking the separated stories—his intrusion reorients and recasts our roles from one of antagonist in a tragedy to being a hero in a tragic-comedy. Often God's role is as an off-stage presence whose coming sets all the other action into motion, yet whose absence requires all the other characters to become more alive and attuned to their humanity. Whatever the role God chooses, he enlivens, disturbs, and sets us into motion to engage both his absence and presence. We inevitably are playing off God as we each attempt to find our voice and discover our role.

Whatever the role God chooses, he enlivens, disturbs, and sets us into motion to engage both his absence and presence.

ACTING WITH GOD

We love drama—just not our own. We like to watch the fall of politicians who have sexual trysts with prostitutes, and even more we love the power of voting for the singer or dancer who most deserves to make their way to the next round of success. We are voyeurs who delight in vicariously participating in the drama of reality television, sports, office gossip, or magazines that pander to our desire to see and know celebrities. Yet we can't escape the daily dramas that impinge on our character.

We are on a stage not of our choosing, and often not of our desire. We are constantly called to speak and to act in order to move our drama forward, even when we don't like the script. In doing so, we begin to discover the complexity of the plot and the tragic knot that makes the story line difficult to live. Balthasar wrote, "Man is placed on the world stage without having been consulted; when the child learns to speak, it is being trained to perform its part: Is this role prescribed, or can it choose and fashion it itself? No one can respond to a question—a cue—without having identified himself, at least implicitly, with a role." It is the question "Who am I?" that "the actor must answer, whether he wishes to or not, either before the play begins or as it unfolds."[3]

We discover who we are as the play proceeds. Our roles becomes clearer as we act and choose one course rather than another. The plot thickens, and more is required of us. Who we are at our best and worst rises in the midst of the extremity of the drama. God joins our play; we act out our parts with him. The interplay takes the story, somehow, in directions that the audience or the actors could not have conceived. The progress may have a well-written script, but before the play ends, God will have required us to move from the conventional script to improvisation. God demands we create in order to discover ourselves and the core of the characters we are meant to offer the audience.

You and I are cast in a role, yet we are equally called to create that role onstage in the presence of other actors who, too, are called to do the same. It might be viewed as chaos, but in fact it is the rarest of privileges: engaging chaos to discover the true nature of a new coherence that could not have been found without the mess of disorder. Disorder helps us face the core rituals and symbols that no longer give meaning to our lives and open the possibility of new ways of being. Fritjof Capra wrote,

"Science will refer to these chaotic places as 'points of instability' where dramatic and unpredictable events take place, where order emerges spontaneously and complexity unfolds."[4]

Disorder helps us face the core rituals and symbols that no longer give meaning to our life and open the possibility of new ways of being.

I sat with a rare and mighty actor who stepped on the stage of addressing the sexual harm his mother had done to him as a young child. Her abuse involved chronic presentations of her unclothed or barely clothed body and requisite massages and touch that bound him to her. He had been in flight for decades as he advanced in a field that required immense technological knowledge and even greater personal risk to serve his clients. He is a warrior—driven, consumed, and wild. He was never a man at peace. The rituals of his life involved working endlessly with no rest or beauty for himself. He bought his wife a nice car, but he drove a clunker. He blessed his family with the symbols of wealth and privilege, yet he refused to enjoy any symbol of his success.

To tell him to take a day off was absurd, and it was beyond incomprehensible to consider the Sabbath. Delight was fused with the erotica of abuse, and its ambivalent amalgamation brought him immense shame that could only be (partially) silenced through constant motion.[5] Seldom do we honestly ask, why wouldn't I want to take a day to delight in goodness? Often there are ample reasons that silence, play, and delight are seen as undesirable by many, and by some, as torture. This remarkable man refused to enter the realm of delight because it brought back too many memories of the pleasure he had known with his abusive mother. Even a small dollop of delight requires us to face why we are so afraid of it.

My friend buzzed through his life, seldom ever turning to look behind him and too frantic to slow down for fear of what might overtake him. At one point, he told me, he was so overwhelmed with life he put suicide on his to-do list, but was too busy to do it.

His life was disrupted through various friends and conversations that eventually enabled him to name his abuse. The result was not only a growing capacity to honor the story he hated but to love the drama he was called to live. He eventually confronted his mother, and beyond his wildest of dreams she acknowledged her harm. Slowly, ever so slowly, a new and holy relationship is being built.

As he told me the story of redemption, he stopped and said, "Do you want to hear something odd? I put new bookcases in my house." He built the original cases with cheap wood and little eloquence. They were functional and, according to his wife, ugly. They were a symbol of how he had lived his life as a flight from delight. He said, "After all that had happened to create a new relationship with my mom, I couldn't live with something that was so cheap and tacky. I had to celebrate with something beautiful that I could look at daily and remember God's goodness."

Somehow the bookcases had to be changed—the old book-case was a symbol of his hatred of delight, and he needed to create a symbol that revealed the beauty of his courage and the wonder of his mother's repentance. So it is for anyone who is courageous enough to celebrate the Sabbath. We can't endure life as it is/was, when the Sabbath calls us to imagine what eternity will one day be. We must attempt to capture the beauty of the Sabbath in transformative symbols and rituals that become the props, costumes, and stage for the drama of Sabbath.

SETTING THE STAGE:
SABBATH RITUALS AND SYMBOLS

Sabbath rituals and symbols are the way we act out the drama of a holy, redeemed day. Symbols might include candles or setting the table with our finest china. A ritual may be Sabbath sex or a long, meandering walk in the woods. However we write the script, it is for the sake of creating and joining in the drama of the day.

Through the millennia, many Sabbath symbols and rituals have been given to us by countless different traditions that are of invaluable use in our practice. It is arrogant to ignore the past and its gift of tradition; it is foolish to embrace past symbols as our own if they don't, at some point, bear lavish meaning. There are no symbols or rituals that are so necessary that if violated or forgotten will ruin the Sabbath. We are, again, free to borrow, synthesize, and/or create new symbols. I'd suggest that the key symbols and rituals are meant to offer a condensed experience of peace, abundance, and joy.

PEACE

A Jewish Sabbath often begins with lighting two candles. The candles are a small, fragile presence of light, fragrance, warmth, and invitation. They don't let the surrounding darkness speak the final word. My wife lights our Sabbath candles. Often in Jewish homes the woman lights the candle as the one who represents the arrival of the queen of Sabbath. The candles are lit before darkness comes as a sign of invitation to the queen that the home is prepared for her arrival. In my family's observance of the Sabbath, we pray, sometimes with traditional Sabbath prayers and at other times calling out extemporaneously for what our hearts most need in this time of play.

My wife and I will at some point bless each other. She has pondered my week and our interactions and crafts words to name what glory she has seen in me during the suffering of that week. It is a gift that I find so delicious to have opened for me.

Usually, we have shopped prior to the night and worked together to create a menu I can cook. As I explained earlier, this season has been my opportunity to learn how to cook and to develop the ability to prepare savory meals for our evening and to use the leftovers for Sunday lunch and dinner. The tender care my wife offers in her kind instruction is a gift of peace. Peace must include activities that bring counterpoised tastes, fragrances, sounds, textures, and images into a union of delight.

Peace must include activities that bring counterpoised tastes, fragrances, sounds, textures, and images into a union of delight.

Perhaps it is painfully obvious, but for us, the Sabbath is not a night to watch television or to descend into comfortable chairs and breeze away the evening in a tired stupor reading a magazine. Peace is not an absence of conflict or tension; it is the union of distinctly different things into a whole that is far, far greater than its parts.

What might symbolize diversity and difference being brought to new levels of harmony? Why not invite those with whom you differ on any issue into your home for a meal and ask them to walk through the process they traveled to come to what they believe? Peace calls not for agreement, but hospitality and care; not debate, but sufficient care and curiosity to listen to the different paths people have taken to find meaning.

Peace might involve working on a canvas together with your family, seeing what you create when you each work to make something together. My wife and I worked on a sand tray used with play therapy with children. The process was, of course, fascinating, especially with a dear friend who helped us interpret what we created. All one must do is to ask—what can we do to play in the midst of peace?

We have friends who are musical, so their Sabbath often begins with a gathering of those who play instruments and sing. What they create in the span of hours of intersecting rhythms and syncopation is one of the highest and best symbols and rituals of peace I know. I can only tap my foot, slightly off rhythm. Yet the privilege of delighting in their musicality has been enough to send me to the consideration of taking up the Jew's harp.

ABUNDANCE

I know a woman who buys something new and expensive at least once a week—a scarf, boots, jewelry. She works hard and sees it as a small benefit for her demanding week. I remarked on how she never seems to wear the same thing twice. She looked at me as if I had said the sun usually rises in the east. She said, "Well, it is one of the benefits of working so hard." There was no delight in her words, only the gristle of self-righteousness. If you get what you deserve, then it is impossible to be grateful.

To get what you are owed is merely to balance the scales of justice. If I buy a new watch and pay several hundred dollars and then open the package and find a watch that I know costs twenty-five dollars, I will feel cheated and angry. Justice has been violated. If I opened the same package and saw a watch that cost thousands of dollars and knew it was not a knockoff, I'd be stunned and call the owner and say there has been a significant mistake. If he said, "No mistake. We wanted you to have the watch we gave you," how would I feel? Justice has not been served again, yet this time I'd be overwhelmed with gratitude because I received an unexpected and undeserved gift.

Jesus says, "'The Sabbath was made for man, not man for the Sabbath'" (Mark 2:27 NIV). What symbols will enable you to enter the day with gratitude and not mere luxury? A common means to start the Sabbath is the Shabbat meal. The ingredients should be the finest one will eat all week long. It is one meal to dine with abandon. If you can serve wine, it should be chosen for what would best accent the meal and be of sufficient quality that one could only blush if asked what it cost. All of this requires study and trial and error. We are meant to partake of bounty, and seldom does this have to do with the amount of food or drink we consume. In fact, I'd argue the better the meal, the less one needs to eat if it is truly savored.

The meal should be made festive with one's finest china, tablecloth, and napkins. But pause for a moment: my best Sabbaths have been in the homes of those in Africa who were working to combat the sex slave trade. They are often poor and live in impoverished settings. The meals may not bear the abundance of a Western banquet, but their sacrifice is far better than if I were drinking an expensive bottle of wine. On the other hand, may there be an occasional Sabbath when you drink a bottle of wine that costs more than what you might normally spend on wine in a month.

One symbol of abundance for me is an exquisite Montblanc fountain pen. I write with it only on the Sabbath. I usually reserve a portion of the last few hours of Sabbath to sit at my desk, smoke the best pipe tobacco I own, and take out my pen and leather-bound notebook. It is not a journal, or at least not a traditional journal. I write out on a few pages what I am aware of being grateful for that week. I write in the best penmanship my scrawl will allow and account for the rare and sweet gifts of grace that have been lavished on me that week.

Abundance is waiting to be plucked like lush fruit on a tree—all it requires is the willingness to delight in its plump fragrance and eat. We must develop a taste for abundance on the Sabbath, or we will not be prepared for the glory that is ahead.[6]

JOY

The symbols of joy interplay with peace and abundance. It is impossible to imagine shalom separated from abundance and, in turn, joy. Joy, however, involves primarily the icon of the face. "I could have no greater joy than to hear that my children are following the truth" (3 John 4). We can taste peace in music, abundance in food, and happiness in success or good favor—but joy, at its core, is relational and redemptive.

Joy recognizes in the face of the other the presence of God.

Those with clear sight can see God's face in strangers and ene-mies; most people barely see the face of God in those we love. It requires eyes that are attuned to the rhythms of wonder and worship, not work or worry. One of my pastors, Paul Schuler, says often, "I want to worship more and worry less, work less and worship more." If I am worrying, I am not full of wonder; if I am only working, I am far from worship. I will not see glory in the face of another if my head is down, focused on work, and my heart is full of worry.

Eyes of wonder enable me to anticipate joy with others. Wonder allows one to suspend disbelief to see what is on the stage being acted out as true. Eyes that see work as the true truth only see reality from the vantage point of what is left to do and how far it is from being finished. It is easy to look at our children, students, friends, and spouses from working eyes. We fail to see the glimmers of glory that shine on the edges of the stage.

Joy requires setting aside work for wonder and worship for worry—in order to see the sweetness of what is rather than the disappointment in what is not. For that reason, Sabbath joy requires symbols and rituals that remind us of the joy of redemp-tion. For many episodes, my wife and I were faithful followers of the *Extreme Home Makeover* television series. Our Sabbath ended before Ty shouted, "Move that bus!" but it was an epilogue that sweetened the sadness of Sabbath ending. I am desperate to see redemption grow in front of my eyes over an hour.

*Sabbath joy requires symbols and rituals that
remind us of the joy of redemption.*

One of our rituals is to see a film at least once a month on
the Sabbath that sings loudly of the glory of redemption. It does
not have to be an uplifting family movie; it simply has to tell the
truth that love is stronger than death. Our whole family saw
the movie *Juno* about teen pregnancy and the feisty passion of the
heroine to live with integrity for the life of her child.

Afterward, we discussed how we would have lived together
if any of our children had conceived a child before marriage. It
was hypothetical, and at times the discussion was painful as my
failure of love in lesser struggles was named, but the evening
was sweet with redemption as we all talked about the goodness
and growth we saw in one another to love with less judgment
and more joy.

Rituals and symbols require us to enter the theatre of our
lives and the lives of others with the sense that we are involved
in a far greater play than we can see in this moment. On the
Sabbath, we live as if redemption in our relationships is truer
than all the division, destitution, and despair that exist on the
other six days. We cannot make joy come, nor can we pretend
to be flooded with wonder, but we can put ourselves in our theater seat, clutch our program, and anticipate the rise of the
curtain and the magic that is about to begin.

10

SABBATH SILENCE

SILENCE IS GOLDEN, AND SILENCE IS HAUNTING. THERE may have been a time when silence was appreciated, but we live in an age that is noise bound. Our quiet spaces are filled with television, radio, CDs, iPods, and other noise machines. For many, if there is a hint of silence, it is quickly filled with a busyness accompanied with a sound track for our lives that gives it pulse, rhythm, and meaning.

We don't like quiet, until we are glutted with cacophony and need a respite. My wife and I were in Manila for a week, and the crowds and noise were intriguing until I became overwhelmed. We were visiting a downtown market with thousands of voices beckoning us to buy their products, especially discounted, just for us. I was fascinated, yet after an hour I felt my head spinning. I knew I had to escape the noise to keep my sanity. We found a relatively quiet coffee shop, and for a significant time I began to work myself out of the noise that enveloped me.

In some ways, silence can be as disconcerting as the roiling noise of a bustling urban center. Silence sets the stage for the dramas of our lives to come into full view rather than standing in the shadows. Consider how often you turn on the radio when you get into a car or the television when you arrive home at the end of the day. Or how music plays in the background—in elevators, restaurants, or when we are put on hold on the phone. What would happen if we said no to noise? Not that the Sabbath is meant to be a day of quiet and repose as it is often slated to be, but what would happen if a portion of our Sabbath, or an entire Sabbath every quarter were spent in quiet?

The Sabbath is like every other gift—it requires practice and discipline to grow in delight. For many, a day, or even a portion of a day spent in silence would seem like a divine time-out, or punishment rather than a gift of joy. It may be that the drama of silence has not captured our hearts yet as a gift.

The Sabbath is like every other gift—it requires practice and discipline to grow in delight.

THE STILL, SMALL VOICE

The drama of silence is that it is the stage where God shows up more frequently than in the bustle of our busyness. It is foolish to say that God doesn't show up in noise—God can show up whenever the Father, Son, and Spirit wish to do so. Yet if there is a time and place for us to hear the voice of God, it is in the midst of quiet.

Then again, God may not show up at all when we set the stage for his arrival. It is as simple as God is God, and God shows up when God wants to do so, not when we arrange for him to appear. There are too many times in my life that I expect God to speak in a manner that is not much different from a horoscope or a fortune cookie. I want answers; I want help; I want mystery—on my terms. Somehow God seems to know when I am bent on making him in my image and is peculiarly unresponsive to my idolatrous manipulation. Yet God speaks, and often it is in the midst of allowing my heart to hear the massive volume of noise present in my silence.

It is obvious—noise masks a far greater cacophony that will seldom be heard until we choose silence. The problem is the underlying noise is louder than the masking sounds we use to cover what we don't want to hear. If we dare to listen to those voices or sounds, then we must be open to being deeply disturbed. Most of the time, it is the voice of regret or worry that ascends and snarls at the freedom of wonder and worship. To let the voices speak, to urge them to get louder and more dramatic is counterintuitive. They slime us from their hidden, dark corners. To cast light on their intrigue and malevolent intentions is to steal some of their power.

Further, to name the face that comes with the voice pares its power even more. The voice may be the angry sentinel that condemns you every time you slow down and ponder the terrain you have covered. Whose face goes with that sentinel—father, coach, mentor, abuser? Ultimately, the force behind all accusations is the evil one and its hoard of foul minions. Silence sets the stage to see all the actors attempting to hijack the drama.

What I have described so far is the labor that needs to go on during our six days of work, and not during Sabbath play. If we attempt to do the hard work of raising the voices to a high din to expose their foolishness, we will be seduced from Sabbath play. We must enter silence to confront the foul and foreign voices before Sabbath. It is part of the preparation before the Sabbath to put aside the division, destitution, and despair of the week. But we can enter into this rich silence only if we are less afraid of the silence that intensifies the dark voices during the other six days.

> *We must enter silence to confront the foul*
> *and foreign voices before Sabbath.*

However, it is important to remember the evil one is no more limited on the Sabbath than it is any other day. But it particularly delights to ruin the one day that eternity utters to give us a sweet taste of the coming and already present kingdom of God. It is foolish to forget one's enemy during this exquisite day of peace.

VOICES OF EVIL

You may be familiar with how evil takes over the voice of those who regularly harm our hearts. Much like the movie *The Matrix*, those selected to guard the secrets of the Matrix can take over the body of anyone they wish and if killed simply find another body, so evil will intone its contempt through any voice that mirrors its purposes. The two central voices it uses are contempt and loss.

CONTEMPT

Contempt sears; it is a sneer that remains in our minds as a judgment that condemns us to endless isolation. We are not fit company—not sufficiently smart, cool, lovely, good, compe- tent, caring, sincere, or authentic—to warrant love. Contempt snickers at the actual or perceived blemish, the mark that sep- arates us from others. The mark may be visible or hidden or merely imagined, but its power is that it provides an explana- tion for why we suffer loneliness.

The contempt of others is often joined by our self-con- tempt. We judge ourselves even more severely than our ene- mies. Our enemy starts the fire, but we add the fuel. The blaze consumes our remaining dignity, until we are tired of the voice of accusation resounding in our heads—then, we get busy and noisy. We silence the accusations with the five thousand songs on our iPod that play in a random, unpredictable order.

I returned from a class at Mars Hill Graduate School to

write, and the face of a student kept crowding into my work. She had sneered through most of the class. In a moment where other students were laughing, she glared at her peers as if they were fools and then rolled her eyes with adolescent flair. As I wrote, I found myself forming sentences to silence her disdain and then berating myself for her effect on me. *I have taught for nearly thirty years; why would one impertinent, mocking face haunt me?*

The levels of irrationality go far beyond what I have written. Even at this writing, I am not clear what is unnerved in me by her face when others who bear far more weight in my life have turned against me with less effect. However, I am clear that evil wants to use her disdain to cancel any good I might have done or may do and to convince me it is time to depart from the messy work of interacting with people.

It is stunning to look at the power of contempt. From one disdainful student I am contemplating retirement. The fact that I could be so ill affected indicates that I am wickedly disturbed and ought not to be in the classroom. Then the fact that I'd think about quitting at all proves I am a quitter and ought to quit. It is an endless sequencing of convoluted logic and the violence of contempt. And it is magnified by the delight of evil that it has far more power to move the soul than the apparently far lesser power of kindness.

Silence enables us to see the characters on the stage who are antagonists decidedly committed to robbing us of delight. We must name the content of their accusations and understand the descent into hell that contempt propels. Then and only then can we silence the noise of contempt to hear the small, still, kind voice of God.

LOSS

A second voice that will often surface with silence is loss. Loss is the voice of destitution. It is a grief we feel too impoverished to invite in as a guest, so we send it away as an unwanted stranger. Just as we must turn up contempt to hear what it is really saying, so we must increase the volume on loss or it will be a siren that chronically calls us away from grief, and therefore from joy.

Before my wife and I went on sabbatical for six months, my boss, academic dean Keith Anderson, called me to his office and asked me if I was ready for my sabbatical. I told him our itinerary and what I intended to read. After I finished, he asked again, "Are you ready for what will come?" I finally had enough wisdom to ask, "What are you asking that I am not getting?" He said, "Most people don't expect the amount of loss and grief that surfaces when you are finally quiet." I was not ready for his question, remark, or the coming grief.

He reminded me of what I knew—most start-up organizations are fraught with untimely departures, chaos, mountains of blame, monumental mistakes, heartache, exhaustion, and loss. He then prayed that our sabbatical would be the beginning of owning the loss and grief associated with the startup of Mars Hill Graduate School.

During our first three months, I found myself awakened from a deep sleep weeping—unaware of the content of the tears, other than I felt shadowed in sorrow. Grief is similar to vomiting. At its deepest convulsion it exhausts, nauseates, and relieves. It empties us, weakens us, and prepares us for food that in due season will strengthen us. But in its immediate aftermath, we need rest.

For many, the discomfort of a churning stomach is less noxious than vomiting—and so illness works itself out far more slowly, if at all. Grieving releases the toxins of loss and invites comfort. "Blessed are those who mourn, for they will be comforted" is not a principle, it is a promise (Matt. 5:4 NIV). But the comfort that comes with mourning is not a palliative—it doesn't take away pain; instead, it offers the grace not to refuse the sorrow. Comfort reminds us we are not alone, even if it doesn't take away the loss.

Grief is to be entered the other six days, not on the Sabbath. What grief we may feel or enter on that day needs to be postponed but not denied. The Sabbath may well be the day we hear the voices of accusation or loss, but only long enough to choose to listen to the louder voice of commendation, not contempt; and to comfort, not loss.

SWEET SPEECH

Sabbath silence opens the heart to meditation and prayer. These doors are openings to enter into a holy time to hear God.

SABBATH MEDITATION

To meditate is to chew something over in your mind until it runs wet and sweet into your heart. The word itself is used to describe a cow chewing its cud. The cow turns it around and around until the grass is digested and the nutrients are absorbed.

One Sabbath, my wife and I took our ritual walk and talked about the death of her mother and father. Both her parents, at times, could be highly critical and disdainful, and I asked her how she had come to be so kind. The conversation lasted for a half-mile, but after a while we both settled into quiet. I began to meditate on kindness. I masticated kindness.

The first flavor that filled my mouth was the phrase "God's kindness leads you toward repentance" (Rom. 2:4 NIV). It is still a shocking phrase for me. I pondered how God's kindness has given me opportunity to repent. My mind scanned a dozen events and settled on one. Why this one? I have no idea, but it was clear that my heart found this moment compelling.

The memory was the first time I entered the home of my best friend Tremper Longman and met his mother, Mernie. I shook her hand as she stood in front of her refrigerator. We may have talked for a minute or more, and in the middle of the conversation, I put my hands on her sides, lifted her in the air, and put her down near the stove. I then opened the refrigerator door and rummaged around for some food. After I had removed a plate of ham, she asked if I wanted bread for a sandwich.

Her eyes twinkled with delight and humor. She was not

unnerved by my decidedly boorish behavior but was instead ready to play. Within weeks I found her a strong advocate, a formidable opponent, and a gift of divine kindness. I was smitten. I still am by her kindness.

Meditation is a form of reflection that allows us to intersect the script of our lives with texts that bring new meaning and perspective. New connections can't be seen without a willingness to be intrigued and confused. How did she know not to get perturbed? Why did I feel so comfortable with her from the beginning? What did she know that allowed her to be so unpredictable? To remember and meditate is to open one's heart to God by praying, "What do you want me to know, to hear, and receive from you?" Meditation is meant to prompt prayer.

SABBATH PRAYER

Prayer is a conversation with mystery. I could rightfully say prayer is conversation with God, yet it seems there are times where if God hears, he doesn't answer, or even seem to be present. Prayer is no less than a conversation, but sometimes it is so one way that it seems best to call it an encounter with mystery. Sometimes my words are all I hear as they reverberate in an empty room and against a gray, silent sky. There are other times my cry is muffled against God's chest, and I feel surrounded by strong arms. God may be unchanging, but with me the Trinity offers ongoing novelty.

Sabbath is a threshold we cross into eternity; therefore,

prayer takes on a different tone than on the other six days. Prayer is multifaceted—even the Lord's Prayer is but one model rather than the "right" way to pray. The Lord invites us to pray for our daily bread. But God's people were given on the day before the Sabbath two measures of manna so they would not need to work for their food (Ex. 16:22–30).[1]

It is not wrong to petition God on the Sabbath, but the heart of the Sabbath is to delight in all he has given us, rather than to ask for what has not yet been fulfilled. Prayer on the Sabbath might well fit into the categories of praise or invitation.

Prayer on the Sabbath might well fit into the categories of praise or invitation.

SABBATH PRAISE

Praise calls out to any who might hear, "Look—be amazed and grateful at the goodness before us." Praise orients us to behold and then bids us to bow before someone, something far greater than ourselves. It is not a compliment; it is a summons.[2]

If we are given a compliment, it is appropriate to say, "Thank you." The compliment is a gift and, if sincere, a pleasure to receive. But heartfelt and indebted praise from someone is beyond our capacity to receive well or for long. It is too humbling.

We can no more receive another's praise than deny it, so we settle by awkwardly saying, "You're welcome." But what we want to say is, "Thank you, thank you, for allowing me to be such a delight in your life." But to say that would be too odd for most. In fact, we long to say is, "Thank you, God, that you have given me the privilege of being part of your glory." All praise is ultimately glory to God.

We are not only meant to praise God, but we are also to praise one another before God. Just as every face on earth is a window into the mystery of God's heart, so every face is meant to receive praise, even our enemies. Sabbath praise is a unique time to bless those who have escorted us to the cross as friends or foes. Sabbath is the day we are to behold the face of the other and speak of the glory we see.

> *Sabbath praise is a unique time to bless those*
> *who have escorted us to the cross as friends or foes.*

David Schnarch, in his book *Passionate Marriage,* argues that sexual joy includes keeping one's eyes open to look into the face of one's lover who is receiving and giving pleasure.[3] The concept often provokes disgust or terror for many couples. It is too intimate. One may share body parts or fluids, but not gaze. Such is the power of shame—it steals our ability to behold and be amazed and grateful. Praise is meant to be given and received with eyes open, irrespective of the discomfort attending the process.

Note that praise given and received from God or from others cuts counter to the power of contempt. One cannot receive praise, even in awkward discomfort or unbelief, without bumping against the noise of contempt. *Is it true? Does my wife really believe I am a good man? Does she really admire me? If she does, and I respect her as much as I do, then why am I drawn to believe a lie about myself and not my wife? And if I believe my wife, then how much more am I to believe God?* Praise offered and received is meant to lead us to another kind of prayer—invitation.

SABBATH INVITATION

The simplest invitation we make to God is to ask, "What is it you want to say?" Few of us believe God speaks. He does. Sadly, it has taken me most of my Christian life to believe something so simple and childlike. My theology argued against God speaking except through the Bible, so I refused to listen for a number of decades. I believed God spoke through his Word by his Spirit—period.

Then I edged closer to the reality that God could speak through many other texts, including movies, art, and sunrises. But I still resisted the simplest hope that he would or could speak directly and unequivocally to me. He had already done so years before I confessed that he could, but I held it off as an aberration not to be considered, let alone acknowledged.

I find such lonely heroics of faith unabashedly cynical and faithless. God speaks. Of course, not always when I want, about what I want to hear. I recall on a Sabbath shouting at him that he was silent and wouldn't tell me what I wanted to hear. He asked me, "Really? Then ask and see what happens!" His words were so loud I expected the universe to stop and look to see who he was addressing. It was not a happy Sabbath, and I turned from him and fled from his invitation. Often I want to hear him until he speaks.

Sabbath prayer is an invitation to God to speak artfully, whimsically, passionately of his love for us. It is not the same as asking him to cover our contempt or fill our emptiness to dispel our despair. Prayer is an invitation to ask God how he delights in us. Will we invite God to join us in Sabbath joy, to dine with us and celebrate?

Will we invite God to join us in Sabbath joy,
to dine with us and celebrate?

At first it may be too stunning to hear God's joy in us or the fullness of his heart for us when we make room to let him speak. We may only be able to hear a few sentences, but there are many Sabbaths to listen, and over time we will hear more and more of his gratitude and desire to be with us. He delights to tell us how utterly and inconceivably wild he is about us.

11

SABBATH JUSTICE

THE SABBATH AND ITS 7X7 PERFECTION, THE JUBILEE, IS the most revolutionary event in the Scriptures. It resets our equilibrium in a world that is chronically imbalanced by the burden of the curse. The Sabbath Jubilee is a holy year, set apart to proclaim freedom:

> "In addition, you must count off seven Sabbath years, seven
> sets of seven years, adding up to forty-nine years in all. Then
> on the Day of Atonement in the fiftieth year, blow the ram's
> horn loud and long throughout the land. Set this year apart
> as holy, a time to proclaim freedom throughout the land for
> all who live there. It will be a jubilee year for you, when each
> of you may return to the land that belonged to your ances-
> tors and return to your own clan." (Lev. 25:8–10)

The Sabbath Jubilee is often said to be as impractical as the Beatitudes. It offers a poetic and ideal perspective on how life should be lived, but it cuts so deep against the grain of practicality that it must be viewed as foolishness.

Life is inevitably unfair. The rich accept it as inevitable; the poor bear it as unjust and unchangeable. Most social structures, especially class designations, are set in concrete and change only due to cataclysm or revolution. When a revolution is violent, it merely changes the veneer, allowing the oppressed to attain new power to enslave those deemed worthy of class punishment.

As the wise teacher in the book of Ecclesiastes tells us, "Again, I observed all the oppression that takes place under the sun. I saw the tears of the oppressed, with no one to comfort them. The oppressors have great power, and their victims are helpless. So I concluded that the dead are better off than the living" (Eccl. 4:1–2). There is hopelessness writ large in these true words, yet there is something more true—the Sabbath. The Sabbath changes the tyranny of injustice and announces in real time that no one is to be left behind in the rut of powerlessness.

All those who serve the powerful, including beasts and land, are set free for a day. It is not a break or a respite to regain strength to live under the yoke for another burdensome six days. Instead, it is a weekly reminder, to all, that injustice and inequality is to be overthrown by delight and joy. To the degree the rich and the poor, the powerful and the powerless, eat, drink, and celebrate the Sabbath, it will be impossible to conduct oneself in the next six days, as if injustice is truer than the Sabbath.

The Sabbath is a time to celebrate repentance and to delight in its fruit—freedom. The Sabbath frees slaves, foreigners, and strangers from the bitterness of their servitude and frees their masters from the corrosive hardening of absolute power. Sabbath is a gift of equality that offers a stunning reversal of the fall:

> "Observe the Sabbath day by keeping it holy, as the LORD your God has commanded you. You have six days each week for your ordinary work, but the seventh day is a Sabbath day of rest dedicated to the LORD your God. On that day no one in your household may do any work. This includes you, your sons and daughters, your male and female servants, your oxen and donkeys and other livestock, and any foreigners living among you. All your male and female servants must rest as you do. Remember that you were once slaves in Egypt, but the LORD your God brought you out with his strong hand and powerful arm. That is why the LORD your God has commanded you to rest on the Sabbath day." (Deut. 5:12–15)

Space inevitably creates levels of hierarchy, power, and privilege. We can work to gain space—we can steal, negotiate, threaten, or bargain to gain more space. We can even buy space. We cannot do so with time. Perceptions about time can be manipulated, but time cannot be wrested from someone the way we can control space. We can gain more space; we cannot create more time for our lives. We can even take a life, but we can't increase our time from the deposit of their life. Time is not in our control.

*The Sabbath is a time to celebrate repentance
and to delight in its fruit—freedom.*

Before time we are all equal—no one has more or less due to their power or position—and death, time's scythe, creates ultimate equality in that no one can escape its amputation. We are called to submit our lives to the Sabbath, which is to bend the knee before the One who submitted himself to time yet is the ruler of time.

The Sabbath frees the slaves, beasts, and land, and perhaps, even more remarkably, it frees the one who falsely believes he is the owner of his servants, flocks, and estate. And then the playful freedom of repentance draws everyone together to eat, drink, dance, sing, and to celebrate.

REMEMBERING SLAVERY

As simple as it may appear, the command is clear—no one, including your sons and daughters, male and female servants, animals, and any foreigners living under your roof is to work. But far more, they are to rest "as you do" (Deut. 5:14).

"As you do" implies equivalence, equality. We are not to ask our maidservants to make a fire on the Sabbath. They are not to prepare our breakfast or get wood for the oven. They are to celebrate and delight as we do. If we intend to celebrate the

Sabbath with a fine calf, then our servants and those foreigners and strangers living under my roof are to celebrate with us. Just as we do, so must all others. And we do so to remember our common history of slavery and our future liberation.

Most of us don't have live-in servants or the financial power to take in a family of foreigners and strangers to bless— so what relevance is this to the middle class? The Sabbath is intended to save us from forgetting our pasts or ignoring our futures. The past is our exodus escape from Egypt; the future is the coming kingdom that has already arrived in Christ Jesus.

To forget our past in Egypt is to deny that we were all once slaves of unrighteousness, and this involves more than personal sin—it includes our allegiance to systems that seem inevitable and unchangeable, but are not. It has been said a thousand times in countless articles and books, but it remains unaddressed: Jesus seldom talks about sexual sin compared to poverty and justice for the poor.

We don't see our economic assumptions—the necessity to send our children to college or the presumption of the divine right to retirement—as indications of our enslavement to systems that have little to nothing to do with the kingdom of God. We remain slaves even if we know personal forgiveness from our sin. The Sabbath is a call to freedom from every remnant of Egypt's idolatry.

The Sabbath is also a promise regarding our future glory in the new heavens and earth, a righteously just and compassionate society. Yet the future is trivialized if the Sabbath is just a day off. It is to be viewed as a day that offers a taste of the radical day of redemptive justice.

The Sabbath is also a promise regarding our future glory in the new heavens and earth, a righteously just and compassionate society.

Many in the middle class look to the suffering of others with a remorseful neglect that says, "I feel sad for them, but I don't know what to do." The suffering of others and the complexity of injustice is just too big to address. So we leave it to the experts and to government. The result is lots of verbiage from the experts and lots of money spent by the government with little to show but waste.

People say, "What can I do as one individual, or one family, to address the plight of the Karen people or sex slave trafficking or AIDS or poverty or methamphetamine use in South Africa or global warming?" The enormity of each issue seems to justify a sad shrug and a collective sigh that signals, "I care, but I am powerless." The Sabbath frees us from both guilt and neglect.

The reason for Sabbath celebration in Deuteronomy is different, though connected, to the Exodus commandment. We are to free the slaves because we were once slaves. Sabbath is a remembrance of the stale bondage of Egypt and the fresh air of our new garden given to us because of the faithfulness of God's covenantal love, not due to our capacity to make God happy. Yet God is more than happy with us—he adores us and lavishes us with freedom and joy.

To remember our slavery frees us to be grateful. But the sneaky part of gratitude is it draws us to a new capacity for discontent. The more I am free of bad food, the more intolerant my body becomes to unhealthy fare. Discontent due to disappointment is usually full of vengeful demands; discontentment that arises from a desire for something more delightful for others is creative and diligent. The more we share with others the glory of delight, the less we can endure the inequality of power and privilege that we hoard and deprive others.

To remember our slavery is to name our chronic battle with addiction, idolatry, and self-obsession. To remember requires that I face that as far as I have come, there is a great distance further to go. But the Sabbath is not about what is left undone; it is about what has already happened. To remember slavery is to feast on the redemptive moment—the now—of freedom.

JOYFUL REPENTANCE

Sabbath celebrates repentance by acknowledging our changes. But far more, Sabbath celebrates the God who frees the heart from slavery. God has not only redeemed us from Egypt, but he has turned our hearts toward eternity. This turn from the past enslavement to the future hope creates a new present. We call this turning *repentance*. Repentance is far more than merely saying, "I am wrong, and I am sorry." It is certainly no less. But it is a radical movement from where we have found life (Egypt) to the hope of the Promised Land, thus enabling us to wander as foreigners and strangers in a land that is not yet our own.

Sabbath celebrates the God who frees the heart from slavery.

The truest fruit of repentance is always hope, even in the face of overwhelming and unrelenting dour circumstances. Hope is not mere optimism; rather, it is moving forward in anticipation of redemption in spite of the improbability of rescue.

The scene in the movie *Glory* where the freed slaves are preparing for their assault on a heavily guarded fortress sings with hope. Not hope of living or winning the battle; instead, the hope that fortifies their song is the glory of being able to choose to fight or not as free men. Whether they lived or died, they were free.

The theologian Jürgen Moltmann wrote, "Man is not liberated from his old nature by imperatives to be new and to change, but he rejoices in the new which makes him free and lifts him beyond himself."[1] The Sabbath turns us to God—it is a day of turning toward God which is the heartbeat of repentance. Further, the Sabbath is the celebration of freedom for ourselves—and if for us, then for all who reside under our roofs.

The Sabbath, therefore, is not merely a day to stop working; it is a day to renounce all activity that impoverishes, enslaves, or demeans others. It is a day set aside not to take or to procure, but to nourish and to give. Indeed, it is a day to dream and to hope. What if the whole earth were to celebrate the goodness of the earth? What if we're to give thanks to the One who created us? What if it were a day of intentional acts of kindness?

The cynic in me scoffs. I gave up such notions once I saw the silliness of the Age of Aquarius. I've seen every form of utopian thought turn greedy and cultic. Idealism has not only gotten me in every conceivable trouble, but it has enabled me to be part of creating structures and organizations that have harmed others, and me.

Yet the day of delight beckons and woos with seductive sensuality and honor, *Will you sanctify me rather than sully me? Will you call me beautiful and holy rather than fritter the day away in banality?* Repentance turns to the Sabbath queen and embraces her music.

FREEDOM TO SING

Sabbath repentance leads to song—literally. It is impossible to think of a festival or a party without singing. Music is a good vibration due to a percussive blow or the movement of strings or metal. It is breath that reverberates in sound, silence, and then repetition. The first and most beautiful musical sound is speech. Mere talking is the movement of breath against vocal chords. The change of pitch and speed creates what most people would call song. But all music is essentially a form of speech that communicates what words alone can seldom translate.

Every culture and every individual makes music, even if it means turning on an iPod. Singing is inclusive and binds us to others we may not know or who even exist in the same century. And Sabbath is not only a song in itself, but it invites us to sing.

> The Sabbath was the music that took the groans of hurt and the words of hope and created a song. The Sabbath song is also a song of inclusiveness, a song that affirms the place for every person in God's family—the resident alien, the immigrant mother, the Korean family that lives next door, the Latino teenager, the man dying of AIDS, the women of all races who know domestic violence, all of society's marginalized. The Sabbath is a sanctuary for the alien, a sanctuary where there is always room for another person, because it is a place in time, not space."[2]

Celebrating the Sabbath is not about being Jewish, Christian, a follower of Baal, or a Buddhist—it is woven first and foremost into creation as a way of being that is true for all people whatever they believe. All human beings are created to enjoy the freedom of the Sabbath.

This is not a covert justification for Blue Laws or the requisite demand on civil society to impose monetary or legal consequences for choosing not to partake. That is an unholy alliance between church and state that has belittled both the gift and those to whom it is given. One does not demand compliance; instead, one lives the Sabbath so richly that one would be foolish not to follow.

How do we live out this inclusive song, this call to justice and freedom uniquely on the Sabbath?

JUSTICE: RELENTLESS INVITATION TO PARTY

Justice is usually considered to be the righteous application of law and order against those who misuse power, break laws, and harm others. Justice punishes and corrects the evildoer and warns others from pursuing a similar path. What is problematic in this definition is it neglects the victim and fails to see that grace is the fruit of justice, not its polar opposite.

Grace is not the exception to justice but its fulfillment. Justice merely puts everyone on the same level with no one using unjust power to escape the face of God. Justice in that sense comes as the full glory and righteous power of God rises in ascendancy and deprives all other powers and systems of its presumption and self-righteousness. One day, every judgment made individually and corporately about others will stand naked before the righteousness of God and be exposed as unrighteous. Every use of power will equally stand before the might of God and be judged.

Every person and every system, from the most heinous and evil to the most apparently righteous and God-serving, will be found wanting—all desperately needing mercy. Grace is mean-ingful only to the degree we are found to be desperately in need by the searing righteousness of God.

> *Grace is meaningful only to the degree we are found to be desperately in need by the searing righteousness of God.*

Grace is God's invitation to the possibility of a new garden of glory based on his son's righteous obedience on our behalf. The Sabbath is the childlike play in the new garden because Jesus has humbly and courageously entered the garden of Gethsemane. A new garden party has begun in the Sabbath, and to not play and delight is rebellion against the incarnation, crucifixion, resurrection, and ascension of Jesus.

What does it mean to play in justice and call forth for free-dom for others? Moltmann describes our Sabbath play in these terms: "*Life* as *rejoicing* in liberation, as *solidarity* with those in bondage, as *play* with reconciled existence, and as *pain* at unrec-onciled existence demonstrates the Easter event in the world."[3]

SABBATH DREAMING

We are meant to dream of the new garden party beyond our bor-ders. We are to ask God to help us expand the party. All we need to do is to follow, to obey the inclinations of our hearts. What burdens grow in you for others? What brings you to tears or anger when you see a news report? How do your gifts, talents, and skills align you for something bigger than your own welfare? The danger with gratitude is that it prompts care. The danger with care is that it engenders dreams. Sabbath is a time to indulge dreams.

My wife and I have been in Thailand and witnessed the plight of the Karen people. We were also in Ethiopia and have seen firsthand the suffering of Ethiopian women who by the thousands daily are boarding ships for use as sexual slaves. How we got to these worlds is the result of Sabbath dreaming.

There is no need to ask, "What can I do?" The question is usually a flight from playing in the new garden. Instead, enter the realm of story, the drama of redemption, and see what moves you.

My wife was sent a birthday present, a book by Oddny Gumaer titled *Displaced Reflections*, about the lives of the Burma refugees.[4] We both read the book, wept, and began to dream. Where will the dreams take us? I don't know yet. I simply know it will take us to a realm of freedom that could not be entered for others or ourselves unless we had chosen to ask, seek, and knock in order to enter the party.

SABBATH ACTION

To dream alone is fantasy if it doesn't move the heart to act. After reading *Displaced Reflections* and perusing the Partners

World Web site (www.partnersworld.org), we gave to the "5 Alive" campaign. This plan asks for fifty dollars to be used to keep five Burmese refugees alive for a month. It isn't a lot to ask. Their Web site also offers beautiful Karen arts and goods for gift giving. Why spend money at your local mall for gifts that say nothing about justice and mercy? Instead, a gift from an IDP (Internally Displaced Person) or from a woman escaping prostitution sings of beauty and opens the heart to wear an icon of suffering hope.

Do your children know what an IDP is? Do they consider how some of their birthday presents might bless little boys and girls a world away who survive for a year on less than the cost of the gift? What about your next big birthday party? Do you really want a new surround-sound extravaganza when for the same amount of money a sound system could be purchased for a thriving Karen church that would enable a thousand people to better hear life offered at the party?

The Sabbath commands delight and will not allow futility, guilt, or pressure to trespass on its day. Action is never enough if defined as eradicating the problem. Action is always enough if it is faithful to the call of the moment. Sabbath action involves responding to the relentless invitation to celebrate the Father's generosity and to dance and sing at our welcome home. And who we will end up dancing with and what songs we will end up learning and singing is a Sabbath mystery.

CONCLUSION
DELIVER US ON TO DELIGHT

THE SABBATH COMES TO AN END—TIME PASSES FROM A day of delight to six days of labor. And it is labor. We suffer the birth agony of hope and despair; the rise of light and the descent of darkness. The night masks the unfinished demands of the day; we surrender to sleep and await the dawn's potential to achieve our dreams. And that day ends for better or worse, yet our desire for what we were most meant to know—delight and glory increases as the week comes to our next Sabbath.

Every human being is in some kind of a weekly war. We strive, fight, retreat, negotiate, and surrender. We crave rest; we thirst for joy. Even those who know the pleasure of Sabbath are seduced to forget the oasis of play that awaits those who give their hearts to Sabbath.

Our war is not with flesh and blood; our reluctance to Sabbath is not a fight with busyness, drivenness, or time. We are caught in and fight battles against delight. Delight unnerves us; God's call to delight terrifies us. To surrender to delight is to hear God's passionate extravagance spoken in a manner that is uniquely crafted for our joy.

Do we really believe that Sabbath delight is God's heart for us? Are we willing to silence the rabble of idols and foul spirits to hear the intoxicating joy of God? We will never know Sabbath delight unless God delivers us from drowning in the noise and grime of our soiled days. Each day may involve countless wars, but every day can also contain the promise of an utterly different eon.

One year ago, Mars Hill Graduate School moved to downtown Seattle, which enabled me to take public transportation to work or to ride my bike. I chose a bike because it the enjoyment of the ride is a gift of the Sabbath to the rest of my week. Every day I ride to work, I am surrounded by the fragrance of the earth, the sounds of creation that are not annulled by the pernicious noise of a radio or suffocated by the enclosed tomb of a glass and metal. Every time I ride, I am reminded of the slower, intentional, sweet pace of the Sabbath. No other day is the Sabbath, but every day can bear a reminder of what is ahead. No other day offers more opportunity for unbound play than the Sabbath, but every day can anticipate with icons, symbols, and rituals the delight that is coming.

My soul needs more than a respite; I need a sanctuary in time. I desperately need to hear the delight of the Father, Son, and Holy Spirit bubble up through the beauty of creation. I crave to hear words of honor and commendation that are oft drowned out by the noise and commotion of industry and labor and lost in the loneliness of abandonment. In the face of stress and suffering and loneliness, I am summoned to sanctify and make holy a day for delight.

The Sabbath is my day; it is our day. We are created to create the sensual rhythms and rituals to taste God's favor. All we must do is to go play in the fields of God and turn our senses to his faithful love. He is ready to play, nourish, and cherish us in a way that is not unlike the other six days, yet is different. How is it different? I don't know. I simply know that it is the day God has created for us to celebrate. It is the one day that we are most uniquely called to play in beauty and freedom. If we ignore or misuse that day, then we are far less human than we could be.

The Sabbath promises that a day of joy is ahead.

The Sabbath is salt and light for the remainder of the week. We are invited to remember the Sabbath all week long and to anticipate its observance ahead. We are invited to hold on to the delight of creation and the wonder of our deliverance from slavery. And to do so in small, incremental ways that remind us the Sabbath is behind us and ahead.

The Sabbath promises that a day of joy is ahead; it is like the fragrant smell of evergreen wafting with a cool spring breeze. Lord God, deliver us all on to delight for the sake of your warming, comforting glory. The queen is coming, and she is almost here. Greet her, and make room in your life for her glory, which is intended for your honor.

NOTES

Introduction: Delight that Delivers Us to Joy

1. Jürgen Moltmann, "The Sabbath: The Feast of Creation," *Journal of Family Ministry* 14, no. 4 (2000), 38.

2. "At a feast there is something is brimming over. That is why guests are invited for a feast, why a chair stands ready for the stranger and why expansiveness predominates. Solipsism and individualism are not appropriate for a feast. This very sin is being overcome. And that gives joy, lightness, radiance." Wiel Logister, "A Small Theology of Feasting," in Paulus G. F. Post, ed. *Christian Feast and Festival: The Dynamics of Western Liturgy and Culture*, (Sterling, VA: Peeters, 2001), 162–63.

Chapter 1: Seldom Sabbath

1. Eugene H. Peterson, "The Good-for-Nothing Sabbath," *Christianity Today* 38, no. 4 (1994). 34.

2. Chesterton would argue the other way—joy is far heavier and thus more fundamental to who we are. Joy is gigantic; sorrow is something "special and small." G. K. Chesterton, *Orthodoxy* (San Francisco: Ignatius Press, 1995), 169.

3. Heschel says that time is inclusive as space is exclusive. See Abraham Joshua Heschel, *The Sabbath: Its Meaning for Modern Man* (New York: Farrar, Straus, and Giroux, 2005), 99.

4. Ibid., 23.

5. "God rests in the presence of his works, for he 'sees everything that he has made,' and finds it to be very good. God directs his shining face toward his creatures and that blesses them and

makes them deeply alive. The Spirit of life always goes out of the living God's shining countenance. When the Creator comes to rest, then the creatures come to themselves and are to bloom like flowers in the sun." Moltmann, "The Sabbath: The Feast of Creation," 39.

6. Concerning the eighth day, Christians "came to believe . . . that Sabbath's meaning had changed within the new creation God began with Christ's death and resurrection. The holy day from now on, therefore, was not the seventh but the 'eighth'—an eschatological day on which the future bursts into the present." Dorothy C. Bass, "The Practice of Keeping Sabbath: A Gift for Our Time," *Living Pulpit* 7, no. 2 (1998), 30.

Chapter 2: Sensual Glory

1. For more on time as a window into eternity, see Abraham Joshua Heschel, *The Sabbath: Its Meaning for Modern Man* (New York: Farrar, Straus, and Giroux, 2005), 73–76.

2. David Bentley Hart, *The Beauty of the Infinite: The Aesthetics of Christian Truth* (Grand Rapids: Eerdmans, 2004), 252–53.

3. I am reminded of a quote by Mike Mason: "I sometimes wonder what it is like for nudists; whether they ever really get used to it. As for me, I still haven't gotten used to seeing my own wife naked. It's almost as if her body is shining with a bright light, too bright to look at for very long. I cannot take my eyes off her— and yet I must. To gaze too long or too curiously is, even with her, a breach of propriety, almost a crime." Mike Mason, *The Mystery of Marriage* (Sisters, OR: Multnomah, 1996), 139.

4. Ruth Haley Barton, *Sacred Rhythms: Arranging Our Lives for Spiritual Transformation* (Downers Grove, IL: InterVarsity, 2006).

Chapter 3: Holy Time

1. The Sabbath is a sanctuary for the alien, a sanctuary where there is always room for another person, because it is a place in

time, not space." Kendra Haloviak, "The Sabbath Song: An Alternative Vision," *Living Pulpit* 7, no. 2 (1998), 41.

2. Marilyn Gardner, "The Ascent of Hours on the Job," *Christian Science Monitor* 97, no. 110 (2005), 14.

3. Ibid.

4. Ibid., 15.

5. Sandra Block, "Off to Work They Go, Even after Retirement Age," *USA Today* (August 31, 2007).

6. As cited in John P. Robinson and Geoffrey Godbey, *Time for Life: The Surprising Ways Americans Use Their Time*, 2nd ed. (University Park, PA: Pennsylvania State University Press, 1999), 25.

7. Abraham Joshua Heschel, *The Sabbath: Its Meaning for Modern Man* (New York: Farrar, Straus, and Giroux, 2005), 99.

8. Ibid., 97.

9. "We speak continually of saving time, but time in its richness is most often lost to us when we are busy without relief. . . . We speak of stealing time as if it no longer belonged to us. We speak of needing time as if it wasn't around us already in every moment. We want to make time for ourselves as if it were in our power to do so." David Whyte, *Crossing the Unknown Sea: Work as a Pilgrimage of Identity* (New York: Riverhead, 2001), 117–18.

10. Lewis Mumford, *Technics and Civilization* (New York: Harcourt, Brace, and Company, 1934), 14–15.

11. Juliet Schor, *The Overworked American: The Unexpected Decline of Leisure* (New York: Basic Books, 1991), 49–50.

12. "What the Puritan dissenting traditions taught was how to spend time, instead of pass time. Now, in the twenty-first century, we are expected to learn how to manage time... since when did time become so unruly that it needed this much managing?" Madeleine Bunting, *Willing Slaves: How the Overwork Culture Is Ruling Our Lives* (London: HarperCollins, 2004), 23.

13. Alexander Schmemann, *For the Life of the World: Sacraments and*

Orthodoxy, 2nd rev. and expanded ed. (Crestwood, NY: St. Vladimir's Seminary Press, 2002), 49.

14. Bunting, *Willing Slaves: How the Overwork Culture Is Ruling Our Lives*, 157.

15. Whyte, *Crossing the Unknown Sea: Work as a Pilgrimage of Identity*. 117–18.

16. Augustine and Hal McElwaine Helms, *The Confessions of St. Augustine: A Modern English Version* (Orleans, Mass: Paraclete Press, 1986), 142–54.

17. Joseph Mali, "Counterclockwise: Notes toward an Ecology of Time," *European Legacy* 3, no. 3 (1998), 13; Brian Edgar, "Time for God: Christian Stewardship and the Gift of Time," *Evangelical Review of Theology* 27, no. 2 (2003), 129.

18. Deborah Bird Rose, "To Dance with Time: A Victoria River Aboriginal Study," *Australian Journal of Anthropology* 11, no. 3 (2000), 288, 295.

19. Heschel, *The Sabbath: Its Meaning for Modern Man*, 59.

20. Ibid., 67.

21. Ibid., 68.

Chapter 4: Communal Feast

1. Eugene H. Peterson, "The Good-for-Nothing Sabbath," *Christianity Today* 38, no. 4 (1994), 34.

2. Jürgen Moltmann et al., *Theology of Play*, 1st ed. (New York: Harper & Row, 1972), 5.

3. As cited in John W. De Gruchy, *Christianity, Art, and Transformation: Theological Aesthetics in the Struggle for Justice* (Cambridge, NY: Cambridge University Press, 2001), 114.

4. Vicki Bruce and Andrew W. Young, *In the Eye of the Beholder: The Science of Face Perception* (New York: Oxford University Press, 1998), 133.

5. David Bentley Hart, *The Beauty of the Infinite: The Aesthetics of Christian Truth* (Grand Rapids, MI: Eerdmans, 2003), 16.

6. De Gruchy, *Christianity, Art, and Transformation*. 111.

7. Belden C. Lane, "Jonathan Edwards on Beauty, Desire, and the Sensory World," *Theological Studies* 65, no. 1 (2004), 46, 52.

8. Diane Ackerman, *A Natural History of the Senses*, 1st Vintage Books ed. (New York: Vintage Books, 1991), xvii.

9. Augustine, *Confessions*, trans. R. S. Pine-Coffin (New York: Penguin Books, 1961), 211–12.

10. Ibid., 238.

11. Brendan Doyle, *Meditations with Julian of Norwich* (Santa Fe: Bear & Company, 1983), 95.

12. Ibid., 97.

13. Ackerman, *A Natural History of the Senses*, 178.

14. David Ford, *Self and Salvation: Being Transformed, Cambridge Studies in Christian Doctrine* (Cambridge, NY: Cambridge University Press, 1999), 267.

Chapter 5: Play Day

1. Jürgen Moltmann et al., *Theology of Play*, 1st ed. (New York: Harper & Row, 1972), 16–17.

2. Ibid., 12–13.

3. Diane Ackerman, *Deep Play*, 1st ed. (New York: Random House, 1999), 4.

4. Ibid., 7–8.

5. C. S. Lewis, *Miracles* (New York: Harper Collins, 2001), 150.

6. Belden C. Lane, *The Solace of Fierce Landscapes: Exploring Desert and Mountain Spirituality* (New York: Oxford University Press, 1998), 178.

7. Ibid.

8. Abraham Joshua Heschel, *The Sabbath: Its Meaning for Modern Man* (New York: Farrar, Straus, and Giroux, 2005), 18.

9. T. S. Eliot, "The Burial of the Dead, Lines 1-7," in *The Waste Land* (New York: Boni and Liveright, 1922).

Chapter 6: Sabbath Play: Division Surrenders to Shalom

1. Abraham Joshua Heschel, *The Sabbath: Its Meaning for Modern Man* (New York: Farrar, Straus, and Giroux, 2005), 29.
2. "It is a serious thing to live in a society of possible gods and goddesses, to remember that the dullest and most uninteresting person you can talk to may one day be a creature which, if you say it now, you would be strongly tempted to worship, or else a horror and corruption such as you now meet, if at all, only in a nightmare. All day long we are, in some degree, helping each other to one or other of these destinations. . . . There are no *ordinary* people. You have never talked to a mere mortal." C. S. Lewis, *The Weight of Glory* (New York: Harper Collins, 2001), 45–46.
3. Norman Wirzba, *Living with Sabbath: Discovering Rhythms of Rest and Delight*, ed. David S. Cunningham and William T. Cavanaugh (Grand Rapids, MI: Brazos Press, 2006), 38.
4. Madeleine Bunting, *Willing Slaves: How the Overwork Culture Is Ruling Our Lives* (London: HarperCollins, 2004), 215.

Chapter 7: Sabbath Play: Destitution Surrenders to Abundance

1. Belden C. Lane, *The Solace of Fierce Landscapes: Exploring Desert and Mountain Spirituality* (New York: Oxford University Press, 1998), 203–4.
2. Eddie Vedder, "Hard Sun," J-Records, 2007.
3. Patrick M and Brown Rooney, Melissa S, *Patterns of Household Charitable Giving by Income Group, 2005* (Indiana University and Google, Summer 2007 [cited May 16, 2008]); available from http://www.philanthropy.iupui.edu.
4. http://www.twobeersbrewery.com.

Chapter 8: Sabbath Play: Despair Surrenders to Joy

1. Lewis Hyde, *The Gift: Imagination and the Erotic Life of Property* (New York: Random House, 1983), 50.

2. Ibid., 51.

3. "Joy is not something one can define or analyze, One enters into joy. 'Enter thou into the joy of thy Lord.' (Matt 25:21)." Alexander Schmemann, "The Proclamation of Joy: An Orthodox View," *Living Pulpit* 5, no. 4 (1996), 8.

Chapter 9: Acting Out Sabbath in Ritual and Symbol

1. Hans Urs Von Balthasar, *My Work: In Retrospect* (San Francisco: Communio Books, 1993), 97.

2. Hans Urs Von Balthasar, *Theo-Drama: Theological Dramatic Theory*, trans. Graham Harrison, 5 vols. (San Francisco: Ignatius Press, 1988), vol 1, 20.

3. Ibid., vol 1, 129.

4. Fritjof Capra, *The Web of Life: A New Scientific Understanding of Living Systems*, 1st Anchor Books ed. (New York: Anchor Books, 1996), 190.

5. "Speed absolves us. . . .When it becomes all-consuming, speed is the ultimate defense, the antidote to stopping and really looking. If we really saw what we were doing and who we had become, we feel we might not survive the stopping and the accompanying self-appraisal. So we don't stop, and the faster we go, the harder it becomes to stop. We keep moving on whenever any form of true commitment seems to surface. Speed is also warning, a throbbing, insistent indicator that some cliff edge or other is very near, a sure diagnostic sign that we are living someone else's life and doing someone else's work. But speed saves us the pain of all that stopping; speed can be such a balm, a saving grace, a way we tell ourselves, in unconscious ways, that we are really not participating." David Whyte, *Crossing the Unknown Sea: Work as a Pilgrimage of Identity* (New York: Riverhead Books, 2001), 117–18.

6. "Unless one learns how to relish the taste of Sabbath while still in this world, unless one is initiated in the appreciation of eternal life, one will be unable to enjoy the taste of eternity in the world

to come. Sad is the lot of him who arrives inexperienced and when lead to heaven has no power to perceive the beauty of the Sabbath." Abraham Joshua Heschel, *The Sabbath: Its Meaning for Modern Man* (New York: Farrar, Straus, and Giroux, 2005), 73.

Chapter 10: Sabbath Silence

1. Exodus 16:22–30, later echoed in the Lord's Prayer (Matt. 6:10–12).
2. "Thanks easily modulates into praise. There the greater the perfection the more repetition is evoked, classically including the repetition of the name of the one praised. To live in a divine presence inexhaustibly creative, wise, good, merciful, and so on, is to find repetition infinitely rich and surprising . . . Praise is in active receptivity which is free within the dynamics of non-identical repetition." David Ford, *Self and Salvation: Being Transformed, Cambridge Studies in Christian Doctrine* (Cambridge, NY: Cambridge University Press, 1999), 155.
3. David Morris Schnarch, *Passionate Marriage: Love, Sex, and Intimacy in Emotionally Committed Relationships,* 1st Owl book ed. (New York: Holt, 1998), 226.

Chapter 11: Sabbath Justice

1. Jürgen Moltmann et al., *Theology of Play,* 1st ed. (New York: Harper & Row, 1972), 44–45.
2. Kendra Haloviak, "The Sabbath Song: An Alternate Vision," *The Living Pulpit* 7, no. 2 (1998).
3. Moltmann et al., *Theology of Play,* 31.
4. For more information about *Displaced Reflections,* go to www.partnersworld.org.

BIBLIOGRAPHY

Introduction

Logister, Wiel. "A Small Theology of Feasting." In *Christian Feast and Festival: The Dynamics of Western Liturgy and Culture*, edited by Paulus G. J. Post, 145–65. Sterling, VA: Peeters, 2001.

Moltmann, Jürgen. "The Sabbath: The Feast of Creation." *Journal of Family Ministry* 14, no. 4 (2000): 38-43.

Chapter 1: Seldom Sabbath

Bass, Dorothy C. "The Practice of Keeping Sabbath: A Gift for Our Time." *Living Pulpit* 7, no. 2 (1998): 16-17.

Chesterton, G. K. *Orthodoxy*. San Francisco: Ignatius Press, 1995.

Davis, Ellen F. "Sabbath: The Culmination of Creation." *Living Pulpit* 7, no. 2 (1998): 6-7.

Heschel, Abraham Joshua. *The Sabbath: Its Meaning for Modern Man*. New York, NY: Farrar, Straus and Giroux, 2005.

Moltmann, Jürgen. "The Sabbath: The Feast of Creation." *Journal of Family Ministry* 14, no. 4 (2000): 38-43.

Peterson, Eugene H. "The Good-for-Nothing Sabbath." *Christianity Today* 38, no. 4 (1994): 34.

Tyndale House Publishers. *Holy Bible: New Living Translation*. Wheaton, IL: Tyndale House Publishers, 1996.

Chapter 2: Sensual Glory

Hart, David Bentley. *The Beauty of the Infinite: The Aesthetics of Christian Truth*. Grand Rapids: Eerdmans, 2003.

Heschel, Abraham Joshua. *The Sabbath: Its Meaning for Modern Man.* New York: Farrar, Straus and Giroux, 2005.

Mason, Mike. *The Mystery of Marriage.* Sisters, OR: Multnomah, 1996.

Tyndale House Publishers. *Holy Bible: New Living Translation.* Wheaton, IL: Tyndale, 1996.

Chapter 3: Holy Time

Augustine, and Hal McElwaine Helms. *The Confessions of St. Augustine: A Modern English Version.* Orleans, MA: Paraclete Press, 1986.

Block, Sandra. "Off to Work They Go, Even after Retirement Age." In *USA Today*, August 31, 2007.

Bunting, Madeleine. *Willing Slaves: How the Overwork Culture Is Ruling Our Lives.* London: HarperCollins, 2004.

Edgar, Brian. "Time for God: Christian Stewardship and the Gift of Time." *Evangelical Review of Theology* 27, no. 2 (2003): 128.

Gardner, Marilyn. "The Ascent of Hours on the Job." *Christian Science Monitor* 97, no. 110 (2005): 14-15.

Haloviak, Kendra. "The Sabbath Song: An Alternative Vision." *Living Pulpit* 7, no. 2 (1998): 40-41.

Heschel, Abraham Joshua. *The Sabbath: Its Meaning for Modern Man.* New York: Farrar, Straus and Giroux, 2005.

Mali, Joseph. "Counterclockwise: Notes toward an Ecology of Time." *European Legacy* 3, no. 3 (1998): 1.

Moltmann, Jürgen, Robert E. Neale, Sam Keen, David LeRoy Miller, and Jürgen Moltmann. *Theology of Play.* 1st ed. New York: Harper & Row, 1972.

Mumford, Lewis. *Technics and Civilization.* New York: Harcourt, Brace and company, 1934.

Robinson, John P., and Geoffrey Godbey. *Time for Life: The Surprising Ways Americans Use Their Time.* 2nd ed. University Park, PA: Pennsylvania State University Press, 1999.

Rose, Deborah Bird. "To Dance with Time: A Victoria River Aboriginal Study." *Australian Journal of Anthropology* 11, no. 3 (2000): 287.

Schmemann, Alexander. *For the Life of the World: Sacraments and Orthodoxy.* 2nd rev. and expanded ed. Crestwood, NY: St. Vladimir's Seminary Press, 2002.

Schor, Juliet. *The Overworked American: The Unexpected Decline of Leisure.* New York: Basic Books, 1991.

Whyte, David. *Crossing the Unknown Sea: Work as a Pilgrimage of Identity.* New York: Riverhead Books, 2001.

Chapter 4: Communal Feast

Ackerman, Diane. *A Natural History of the Senses.* 1st Vintage Books ed. New York: Vintage Books, 1991.

Augustine. *Confessions.* Translated by R. S. Pine-Coffin. New York: Penguin, 1961.

Bruce, Vicki, and Andrew W. Young. *In the Eye of the Beholder: The Science of Face Perception.* New York: Oxford University Press, 1998.

De Gruchy, John W. *Christianity, Art, and Transformation: Theological Aesthetics in the Struggle for Justice.* Cambridge, NY: Cambridge University Press, 2001.

Doyle, Brendan. *Meditations with Julian of Norwich.* Santa Fe: Bear & Company, 1983.

Ford, David. *Self and Salvation: Being Transformed, Cambridge Studies in Christian Doctrine.* Cambridge, NY: Cambridge University Press, 1999.

Hart, David Bentley. *The Beauty of the Infinite: The Aesthetics of Christian Truth.* Grand Rapids: Eerdmans, 2003.

Lane, Belden C. "Jonathan Edwards on Beauty, Desire, and the Sensory World." *Theological Studies* 65, no. 1 (2004): 44-72.

Moltmann, Jürgen. "The Sabbath: The Feast of Creation." *Journal of Family Ministry* 14, no. 4 (2000): 38-43.

Moltmann, Jürgen, Robert E. Neale, Sam Keen, David LeRoy

Miller, and Jürgen Moltmann. *Theology of Play*. 1st ed. New York: Harper & Row, 1972.

Peterson, Eugene H. "The Good-for-Nothing Sabbath." *Christianity Today* 38, no. 4 (1994): 34.

Tyndale House Publishers. *Holy Bible: New Living Translation*. Wheaton, IL: Tyndale, 1996.

Chapter 5: Play Day

Ackerman, Diane. *Deep Play*. 1st ed. New York: Random House, 1999.

Eliot, T.S. "The Burial of the Dead, Lines 1-7." In *The Waste Land*. New York: Boni and Liveright 1922.

Heschel, Abraham Joshua. *The Sabbath: Its Meaning for Modern Man*. New York: Farrar, Straus and Giroux, 2005.

Lane, Belden C. *The Solace of Fierce Landscapes: Exploring Desert and Mountain Spirituality* New York: Oxford University Press, 1998.

Lewis, C. S. *Miracles*. New York: Harper Collins, 2001.

Moltmann, Jürgen, Robert E. Neale, Sam Keen, David LeRoy Miller, and Jürgen Moltmann. *Theology of Play*. 1st ed. New York: Harper & Row, 1972.

Tyndale House Publishers. *Holy Bible: New Living Translation*. Wheaton, IL: Tyndale House Publishers, 1996.

Chapter 6: Sabbath Play: Division Surrenders to Shalom

Bunting, Madeleine. *Willing Slaves: How the Overwork Culture Is Ruling Our Lives*. London: HarperCollins, 2004.

Heschel, Abraham Joshua. *The Sabbath: Its Meaning for Modern Man*. New York: Farrar, Straus and Giroux, 2005.

Lewis, C. S. *The Weight of Glory*. New York: Harper Collins, 2001.

Tyndale House Publishers. *Holy Bible: New Living Translation*. Wheaton, IL: Tyndale House Publishers, 1996.

Chapter 7: Sabbath Play: Destitution Surrenders to Abundance

Rooney, Patrick M and Brown, Melissa S. Summer 2007. Patterns of Household Charitable Giving by Income Group, 2005. In, Indiana University and Google, http://www.philanthropy.iupui.edu/Research/Giving%20focused%20on%20meeting%20needs%20of%20the%20poor%20July%202007.pdf. (accessed May 16, 2008).

Tyndale House Publishers. *Holy Bible: New Living Translation*. Wheaton, IL: Tyndale, 1996.

Vedder, Eddie. "Hard Sun." Music for the motion picture, *Into the Wild*: J-Records, 2007.

Chapter 8: Sabbath Play: Despair Surrenders to Joy

Hyde, Lewis. *The Gift: Imagination and the Erotic Life of Property*. New York: Random House, 1983.

Schmemann, Alexander. "The Proclamation of Joy: An Orthodox View." *Living Pulpit* 5, no. 4 (1996): 8.

Tyndale House Publishers. *Holy Bible: New Living Translation*. Wheaton, IL: Tyndale House Publishers, 1996.

Chapter 9: Acting Out Sabbath in Ritual and Symbol

Buechner, Frederick. *Telling the Truth: The Gospel as Tragedy, Comedy, and Fairy Tale*. 1st ed. San Francisco: Harper & Row, 1977.

Capra, Fritjof. *The Web of Life: A New Scientific Understanding of Living Systems*. 1st Anchor Books ed. New York: Anchor Books, 1996.

Heschel, Abraham Joshua. *The Sabbath: Its Meaning for Modern Man*. New York: Farrar, Straus and Giroux, 2005.

Pieper, Josef, Gerald Malsbary, and Josef Pieper. *Leisure, the Basis of Culture*. South Bend, IN: St. Augustine's Press, 1998.

Tyndale House Publishers. *Holy Bible: New Living Translation*. Wheaton, IL: Tyndale House Publishers, 1996.

Von Balthasar, Hans Urs. *My Work: In Retrospect*. San Francisco: Communio Books, 1993.

———. *Theo-Drama: Theological Dramatic Theory*. Translated by Graham Harrison. 5 vols. San Francisco: Ignatius Press, 1988.

Whyte, David. *Crossing the Unknown Sea: Work as a Pilgrimage of Identity*. New York: Riverhead Books, 2001.

Chapter 10: Sabbath Silence

Ford, David. *Self and Salvation: Being Transformed, Cambridge Studies in Christian Doctrine* Cambridge, NY: Cambridge University Press, 1999.

Schnarch, David Morris. *Passionate Marriage: Love, Sex, and Intimacy in Emotionally Committed Relationships*. 1st Owl book ed. New York: Holt, 1998.

Tyndale House Publishers. *Holy Bible: New Living Translation*. Wheaton, IL: Tyndale, 1996.

Chapter 11: Sabbath Justice

Haloviak, Kendra. "The Sabbath Song: An Alternate Vision." *The Living Pulpit* 7, no. 2 (1998): 40-41.

Heschel, Abraham Joshua. *The Sabbath: Its Meaning for Modern Man*. New York: Farrar, Straus and Giroux, 2005.

Moltmann, Jürgen, Robert E. Neale, Sam Keen, David LeRoy Miller, and Jürgen Moltmann. *Theology of Play*. 1st ed. New York: Harper & Row, 1972.

Tyndale House Publishers. *Holy Bible: New Living Translation*. Wheaton, IL: Tyndale House Publishers, 1996.

Conclusion

Tyndale House Publishers. *Holy Bible: New Living Translation*. Wheaton, IL: Tyndale, 1996.

THE ANCIENT PRACTICES SERIES

PHYLLIS TICKLE, GENERAL EDITOR

Finding Our Way Again by Brian McLaren

In Constant Prayer by Robert Benson

Sabbath by Dan B. Allender

Fasting by Scot McKnight

The Sacred Meal by Nora Gallagher (2009)

The Liturgical Year by Joan Chittister (2009)

The Pilgrimage by Diana Butler Bass (2010)

Tithing by Douglas LeBlanc (2010)

Stand at the crossroads and look; ask for the ancient paths,
ask where the good way is, and walk in it,
and you will find rest for your souls.
—Jeremiah 6:16 (NIV)

THOMAS NELSON
Since 1798